HAUNTED SOUTHEND

Dee Gordon

The
History
Press

To Mum and Dad,
who died in 1992 and 1993 respectively
but are still remembered daily with much fondness

First published 2012

The History Press
The Mill, Brimscombe Port
Stroud, Gloucestershire, GL5 2QG
www.thehistorypress.co.uk

© The Dee Gordon, 2012

The right of Dee Gordon to be identified as the Author
of this work has been asserted in accordance with the
Copyrights, Designs and Patents Act 1988.

British Library Cataloguing in Publication Data.
A catalogue record for this book is available from the British Library.

ISBN 978 0 7524 6082 6
Typesetting and origination by The History Press
Printed in Great Britain

Contents

Acknowledgements

Of the many people who have assisted in my research, many are named in the stories that follow. I would like to emphasise the following as having been particularly helpful: Bill Raymond; Wendy Pullman; Wendy Newby; Elaine Bernard; David Hobbs; Kathy Scott; Bill Fletcher (Westcliff Spiritualist Church); Peter Fox; Noel Kelleway; Wesley Downes; Bradley Vaughn; Pat Gollin; Judy and Suzanne Flynn; Tonio Perrott; Gerald Main at BBC Essex; Martin McNeill at the *Southend Echo*; Martin Astell and Jenny Butler at the Essex Record Office in Chelmsford; Judith and Toby Williams; Susan Redfern; Marcia Fernandes-Gartside; Marian Livermore; Raymond Lamont-Brown; Mark and Rosemary Roberts (authors of *Paglesham Natives*); Janice Kay at Colchester Library and everyone at Southend Library; Ken Crowe at Southend Museums; Lynn Tait; Ron Bowers (spirit photographer); Nicky Alan (psychic medium); Matthew Lloyd; Lon Strickler; Ian Yearsley; Darren Mann; Chris Looker; Martin Eldridge; Gary Congram; and everyone who helped with images at www.cannon.org.uk and www.footstepsphotos.co.uk.

It is also appropriate to thank Matilda Richards and everyone at The History Press for their interest and support in this venture – as always.

Introduction

It is not necessary to believe in ghosts to be aware that there are things outside our understanding. The twenty-first century has left behind the heyday of Victorian ghosts on unlit country roads and in gloomy rooms lit only by oil lamps, but the stories linger on and are still in the ascendancy. Ghost lore is a part of folklore and of local and human history, and its popularity is consolidated not just by English literature, but by the rise in television programmes and websites devoted to ghost-hunting and contact with the spirit world.

One of the difficulties of researching ghosts and the paranormal is that many apparitions are seen by one person at a time and thus are without independent corroboration. So this book is based on published reports and on interviews with witnesses about their experiences, with some second-hand accounts. Some of the published reports and second- (and third-) hand accounts are obviously not always reliable and in some cases are certainly embroidered in the re-telling. This does not mean that the origin, or the core, is not true. Of the many people I met during the research for *Haunted Southend*, not one came across as anything but genuine and honest.

Certainly, I have had the unexpected, and eye-opening, opportunity to meet a clairvoyant, a medium, a spiritualist, and to correspond with ghost-hunters, a psychic medium and a spirit photographer – all outside my normal social remit! This book is intended to report local experiences, to entertain readers, to look into mysteries, and is for everyone with an open mind and a curiosity about life and death. Believers will have their faith reinforced, and the sceptical will have something to think about.

Given Southend's fairly recent appearance as an influential Essex presence – since, effectively, the coming of the railway, prior to which it was merely the south end of Prittlewell the ghost stories within these pages encompass surrounding areas. Some are quite separate entities: from Canewdon, Stambridge and Hullbridge in the north (still rural) to Rayleigh in the west and Foulness in the east, but all are within just a few miles of what is now known as Southend-on-Sea. These villages and suburbs have just as much to offer in the way of the paranormal as does Southend itself – if not more. Also note that, for me, the Southend-on-Sea area includes Leigh-on-Sea, Westcliff-on-Sea and Shoeburyness.

one

Haunted Houses

From little terraced houses to apartments or detached dwellings, the ramshackle to the ostentatious, the following places have stories from the past and the present. In most cases, the locations are identified by the street or road rather than anything more specific, to avoid attracting the ghoulish – and, of course, some have been demolished during the modern re-development of the Southend area. The idea of a house being haunted has different effects on different people. Sutherland Lodge in Prittlewell, for instance, once part of a farm, once a school, and once named Blue House (dating back to 1600) was renamed when it was thought to be haunted, as it was proving difficult to sell. At the other extreme, in 2006, a cottage in Hawkwell was marketed as 'pick up your very own haunted house for a mere £445,000'!

Royal Terrace

In January 1976, Raymond Lamont Brown wrote about the contents of a fascinating journal belonging to his late grandfather, entitled Miss Warren's Essex Ghostbook. One particular chapter (reproduced in the *Essex Chronicle*)

featured a house in this historic location overlooking the town's pier.

Because the journal, which covers the years 1887 to 1893, is handwritten, it is impossible to attribute the origins of this particular haunting to a particular number – it could be No. 1 Royal Terrace, No. 7 or No. 9. What is clear is the reference to a Mr George Martin who was staying in the house during the 1870s, preparing for bed, when the flame of his candle turned suddenly blue. Not only that, he heard a loud clatter, felt the temperature drop, and saw two livid eyes, full of 'pain and utmost devilry'.

Bravely, Mr Martin, as he watched an image form around the eyes, was able to find his voice, asking the intruder 'Who is it? What do you want?' at which the spectre vanished. He informed his host immediately, the latter conceding that this was not the first time he had heard about the ghostly visitation, the difference being that Mr Martin was one of the first to do anything other than flee. The next day the same thing happened, and again Mr Martin stood his ground. The identical sequence of events was repeated, but this time the face was clearer: 'a protruding forehead and dark hair … dark eyebrows … two yellow

Royal Terrace around 1909, little changed today. (Author's collection)

swollen eyelids and cheeks of purple hue surrounded by leprous white. The face stared out of the gloom and glistened unhealthily in the candlelight for several minutes.' He had no opportunity this time of repeating his request, or any other, because the apparition did not linger for long.

This story surfaces again in an article by Wesley Downes in Issue No. 4 of *Essex Ghosts and Hauntings*, the main difference being the attribution of the explanation for the apparition. For Mr Downes, it was the host, or landlord, that revealed all. The host had heard that someone had died of leprosy in that very room some twenty years earlier. Mr Lamont Brown, however, indicates that it was Miss Warren who discovered the history behind the earlier death in the haunted bedroom; but there is no reference to its being leprosy, only a 'strange and then unheard of disease'.

A few yards away is the once-imposing Clifton Court, a red-brick building on the corner of Royal Mews and Royal Terrace. Jessie Payne, in *A Ghost Hunter's Guide to Essex*, writes of a couple who, between

November 1966 and March 1967, had a number of mysterious visitations. The first was a 'grey luminous shape near the end of the bed' which vanished, leaving the room icy cold. Months later, a cowled grey shape, with some facial features visible, appeared in the same vicinity at dawn, but, on being challenged, it again disappeared. This time, an unpleasant, earthy, musty odour was left behind. Although the couple called in a vicar to exorcise the room, they never felt comfortable there and moved out soon after.

Royal Terrace, one of the oldest residential streets in Southend, was built at the end of the eighteenth century overlooking the estuary. It started life as Grand Terrace with a library and hotel at its eastern end, built as added attractions for the genteel. However, it struggled to achieve its aim until Princess Caroline, the wife of the Prince Regent, took over the central dwellings here in 1803: No. 7 as a drawing room, No. 8 for dining and No. 9 for sleeping! It was this visit that resulted in the change of name to Royal, and this surviving Georgian terrace was also visited by Lady Emma Hamilton and Lord Nelson (1803 and 1805). Such history should have perhaps resulted in more romantic ghosts, but their sojourns were probably too brief to leave a lasting impression. Although there is a Lady H room and a Nelson's look-out in the Hamilton's Boutique Hotel in Royal Terrace, plus Princess Caroline and Prince Regent rooms in the Pier View Hotel, there are no reports of hauntings.

Royal Mews

When Tonio Perrott moved into his home in 1988, it needed a lot of work, and he called in an architect to assist him. The architect set about removing an internal wall, which turned out to be five bricks deep, revealing a small room, complete with a wagon wheel … and a skeleton. The skeleton was draped over the wheel as if he had dozed off there and not woken again, and there were still some remnants of clothing, including an ancient cloth cap. Obviously, the police had to be called in, but the mystery of his identity remains unsolved – the assumption is that he was the old man who lived there previously.

It comes as no surprise, then, to hear that this mews cottage has since been haunted by an old man, holding a walking stick out in front of him. His first appearance, on the stairs, gave Tonio's wife quite a fright, but he is now happy to live alone with his ghost, who is a benevolent presence.

Tonio has also been conscious of what appears to be a second, separate, image, which is no more than a black shadow which

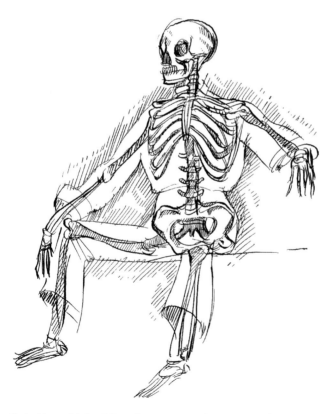

appears at certain times of the month. He can see this shape out of the corner of his eye, and it is always preceded by an intense drop in temperature. A visitor with psychic abilities claims to have spoken to this second spirit, identified as a man in his forties with a malformed hand and a degenerative illness of some kind.

Just before midnight on Christmas Eve, every year, a very special event takes place on the forecourt of this particular dwelling. Tonio and his friends only have to wait a few minutes before they can hear the sound of a horse clip-clopping over cobbles (now tarmac-ed over) and the calls of the coachman, geeing up the horse. The sounds – and the smells, too, of horse and sweat – disappear in

Skeletal image á la Royal Mews. (Image courtesy of www.clipart.com)

Phantom coach and horses from an earlier century.
(Image courtesy of www.clipart.com)

stairs, coming downstairs and into the room where he was sitting, followed by a touch on his shoulder – with, again, no one visible.

On one occasion, his partner, who was sitting in the corner of the room, had also been aware of, and was scared by, the sound of these footsteps entering the room. This prompted her to investigate further.

She went upstairs to ask her daughter if she had been playing in the hall. The girl's answer not only confirmed that she had not been downstairs, but suggested that it could have been the 'other little girl'. When questioned further, the girl described this 'other girl' as being happy, blonde, and as someone who liked to play in the hall and look into the rooms, apparently on a regular basis. As a child, this had seemed perfectly 'normal' to her, not worth mentioning. Further probing revealed that this same blonde girl had been seen by earlier residents.

The earlier history of the house had additional reports of extreme cold in the upstairs back bedroom and on the landing, but this is not necessarily connected to the 'happy girl' seen in the hallway. But what is an unexplained coincidence is a report from a house in Ashburnham Road, very close by, of an identical blonde child laughing and playing in the hall.

the direction of the High Street. What is particularly fascinating about this is the fact that the sounds and smells are witnessed by several people, and it does not occur at other times – Tonio's theory is that the combined energy of a number of people results in this annual visitation.

The mews cottages here were built around 1770, originally as stables for the large mansion-type houses in Royal Terrace. Given their age and provenance, those bricks no doubt have a lot more stories to tell.

Gordon Road

A man who lived here with his family for three years moved in when the owner retired abroad, in around 2004. He knew, before moving in, that the house had a reputation for being haunted, but kept this to himself, even though he too heard movements on the upper floor when no one was there. However, he also heard footsteps on the

Gainsborough Drive

In December 1990, not only the local *Evening Echo* (as it was then called) but the national *Sunday Telegraph* ran a story of a violent pre-Christmas spirit. First the police, and then an exorcist, were called to the house after its occupant had discovered his two-year-old son 'floating' five feet in the air and screaming out for him to look at 'the woman in the ceiling'. The father had thought his son was sleeping until he heard him shouting, and he himself felt 'something' on the stairs on his way up to see to the child.

The police reported furniture having been seemingly hurled across the room, and it was even said that the family dog had been seen flying through the air. The man's wife missed the excitement as she was in hospital, giving birth. Her husband, however, was understandably distraught, and asked the police to call in an exorcist. However, a local chaplain refused to perform this task, fearing that something more violent and uncontrollable might be unleashed.

Although the proceedings were taken very seriously by the police, who confirmed that there was no evidence to suggest that the man had been drinking, there was little that they could do as no crime had been committed. It seems that this was not the first supernatural experience the boy's father had had, and he had in fact sensed a conflict of forces in the house since moving in some three years earlier – between who he suggested was an earlier female occupant (or perhaps her grandmother) and an unidentifiable male. Could the child have been at the centre of some kind of spectral tug-of-war?

Interestingly, a far more rural Gainsborough Drive was where the pregnant Florence Dennis was killed by a gunshot in the head in 1894, a crime for which her lover, James Canham Read, was subsequently hanged; coincidence? Probably – though you never know …

Ronald Park Avenue

Bill Fletcher has been a spiritualist for fifty-two years, so it is not surprising that he has had a number of experiences at his Ronald Park Avenue home. The more receptive you are to sightings, then the more likely you

Fleeting image – make of it what you will. (Image courtesy of www.ghostseen.com)

are to have them. Even during the initial repairs (effected by gas light!) upon moving in, nearly forty years ago, he was aware of 'someone' in the doorway; an opaque, fading image of a smiling woman. It was scary enough to drive Bill out of the building, with chisel and hammer in hand, but when he saw her again on the stairs of the house, he felt that she was merely visiting to see what was going on. This seems to have been confirmed when he described her to his next-door neighbour, and she matched the description of a woman who had lived and died in the house.

Another woman, dressed in a high collar and leg-of-mutton sleeves, appeared clearly at the bottom of his bed at a later date. When Bill awoke, she said 'I'm sorry. I lost direction' and faded from sight. He had seen her quite clearly, and is convinced that she had gone to the wrong house.

There is also a sad tale regarding the death of Emma, his daughter, twenty years ago in a car accident when she was just nine years old – but Emma's spirit has visited Bill to tell him not to be sad, the same words quoted by a young neighbour who also saw her. Emma also told him that she was 'all right now' and she has appeared at the bottom of his bed to ensure that he 'understands' – understands that she had had her time perhaps. It is fascinating to find that the last essay Emma wrote at Chalkwell Infants School was about an accident when she hurt her head, an essay found after her death.

The last time Bill saw Emma was when she made an appearance inside a white opalescent cocoon in the aisle of Westcliff Spiritualist Church a year after her death, wearing a plain white, ankle-length gown hemmed with gold, with a round neck and long sleeves. She just smiled, and Bill, the only one to see her, was happy because he felt that she had made real progress.

Bill's mother had been living with him and his family before her death in the 1990s. His mother had heard her name called in the night, and Bill, too, had seen a nun dressed in white holding her hands out and leading him to his mother's bedroom, again during the small hours, a susceptible time for such visions. So both of them had an idea that her death was fast approaching, and, after her death, Bill observed a white mist rising from her body, forming a ball and moving away, witnessed also by his brother. Bill saw other deceased relatives around the bed at this time, if only briefly, and these relatives appeared to remove the ball of light from the room. His last memory of that day is of the vision of his mother superimposed on her bed, looking bright eyed with newly permed hair, looking in fact as he wanted to remember her rather than ravaged by the disease that finally killed her.

There have also been visitations from Bill's father who died over four years ago. A medium who visited Westcliff Spiritualist Church saw a 6ft-tall man with a military bearing, who spoke to him about a willow casket and funeral arrangements – the description fitted Bill's father. Additionally, the funeral arrangements were accurate as the deceased had saved a lot of willow in his shed which had been put to good use. On another occasion, when Bill's wife was working at night, he heard a sigh and heard the bed creak, with a visible physical depression appearing in the bed. On reaching out, Bill could feel – but not see – the bony frame of his dead father. This, however, appears to have comforted Bill rather than worry him.

Devereux Road

Although this story is anonymous, it has so much detail that it is impossible to ignore. In 1989, the tenant of a flat in this road was awoken by his dog, obviously upset by something unseen in the room, moving from the window to the door. The dog then chased it out of the room, barking, stopping outside a built-in cupboard underneath what had once been a spiral stairway (blocked off some time before 1989).

The dog repeated his barking and 'chasing' on another occasion, when he chased 'something' up to a wall, unable to pursue his quarry any further – and looking suitably puzzled.

But it was not only the dog that had the next experience. The barking woke up his master – and, briefly, a figure of an oldish man with a hat and coat, very close by, appeared, and disappeared. After also hearing footsteps, together with a number of repeat performances from the dog, his owner – now really spooked – began to investigate.

His investigations revealed that the flat above him had also been the location of unexplained sights and sounds, with the electrics going on and off for no apparent reason. Prior to its conversion into flats, the building had once been a school, and this gave rise to a fascinating theory. Because the cupboard and the hallway nearest to it were always cold, although the ends of the hallway were not, the presumption was that someone – perhaps a servant or member of the school staff – had fallen down that defunct spiral stairway and been killed.

This certainly sounds like the ideal explanation. But as to whether there is any truth in it … so often when researching a specific event without information as to dates, the truth is difficult to ascertain. It has been possible to establish, though, that there certainly was a school in Devereux Road listed in Kelly's Directory in the 1930s: St Margaret's Boarding and Day School for Girls.

St George's Park Avenue

In the late 1980s, a husband and wife were doing a lot of structural alterations to their house here, taking out fireplaces etc. They could feel an unhappy presence which made them feel uncomfortable and unsettled, and called in Bill Fletcher from Westcliff Spiritualist Church, and an experienced medium, to see if they could help by exorcising the presence. Upon visiting the house, both Bill and the medium were able to see the figure of an elderly man physically trying to push the couple out – and research indicated that this was

Staircases are popular sites for spooky visitations.
(Image courtesy of www.clipart.com)

the man who had died there. At a subsequent church meeting, Bill was able to talk to the spirit of this man who apologised … it seems that he was simply unaware that he had died, and Bill was not surprised at this, because he feels that this is a fairly common occurrence. Ghosts have a reputation for visiting locations they knew from their earth-bound existence. Bill explained that they do not move around, but materialise from the past into the present.

Victoria Avenue

The *Southend Pictorial* of 1 July 1966 gave an account of police being called to Westborough High School. There they interviewed several sixteen-year-old girls about the events they had reported in an empty house opposite the Priory Park gates (on the corner of Fairfax Drive), concealed from the main Victoria Avenue by overgrown bushes.

One of the girls gave a clear account of the group's unauthorised visit to the house, prompted, it seems, by curiosity. When they were looking around, one girl became hysterical and began to bang her hands against a window, cutting herself in the process. She eventually managed to tell the group she had seen a man dressed in black holding a woman's head down in a tank of water, a much scarier proposition than the figure seen by several other girls – a woman with long blonde hair walking aimlessly around.

As a result, a squad car was sent to the house, Bridge House, which was due to be demolished soon after. Unsurprisingly, they found nothing of consequence. The girls were warned to keep away, but had no desire to repeat their visit.

Lancaster Gardens

When Bill Fletcher was a young man living with his parents in Southend, he liked to listen to what was then modern popular music, and has a special memory of one favourite song by Marvin Rainwater with a line that goes, 'Tell her my journey is over'. He recalls it particularly because he heard it being sung at home by a female voice, and assumed it was his mother at the other end of the house in the scullery, up to her elbows in soapsuds washing the dishes. When he queried his mother's song choice, however, she denied singing the song, but very soon afterwards received a telegram regarding her own mother's death. It was his grandmother's journey that was over – so was it his grandmother singing?

Sutton Road

In 1967, members of a family in one of the council-owned houses became aware of unexplained footsteps, a disembodied voice, and mysterious noises, but thought little of it. That was until their four-year-old son saw what he described as an old man. It seems that, over time, the boy and the old man became friendly, with the man waiting for the boy at the bottom of the stairs and climbing the stairs alongside him.

His mother had some reservations about the boy's stories until she was tucking him into bed one night, when she heard her name being called, and felt that someone else was in the room. After saying goodnight and going downstairs, she heard her son scream out that there was a man in his bed – and she ran back to find the bedclothes scattered and the boy waving his arms around, obviously upset by what had happened.

This event, backed up by visitors to the house mentioning the rocking horse starting to rock violently of its own accord, and of seeing items of clothing fly down the stairs, sent the boy's mother to the local spiritualist church. A medium came to visit, and diagnosed the spirit as that of a First World War veteran who used to live there, who had returned from the battlegrounds to find his wife missing (she was in hospital). This spirit was contacted by means of a séance and he was asked to leave the family in peace, which he agreed to do, after saying goodbye to his friend, i.e. the little boy.

Thus ended the footsteps and the voices, and the boy gradually forgot his 'old' friend.

Chalkwell Avenue

In the 1980s, Barry Sparrow was working as an electrical contractor, and one of his more memorable jobs was the re-wiring of a large house in this prestigious location. It was an unusual dwelling with a minstrel's gallery in a prominent corner position. Three electricians and a decorator spent a month in the house, and, unusually, all of them heard footsteps on the upstairs floor when they were seated downstairs having their lunchtime sandwiches and flask of tea. As no one else was supposed to be in the house, which was uninhabited, one of them went to investigate, but no one was found.

There was more to come. The decorator had brought in his young Alsatian rather than leave him home alone, and the dog stopped eating his own 'lunch' very abruptly, fixing his gaze on an empty corner and barking continually although nothing could be seen – he would not stop barking until his owner had removed him from the room.

A third incident confirmed that there was something going on in this house, which none of the workers involved in its renovation could explain other than by using the word 'haunted'. Barry himself was working upstairs in the eaves, accessed by a small door through a stud wall. The eaves were convenient to run the necessary cabling, but they were pitch black, necessitating the use of a torch. He had not been working there for long, when he felt a sudden icy wind, although it was calm outside, and, in any case, there were certainly no gaps in the outside or stud walls in the vicinity. Not only that, but the wind was strong enough to knock the torch off the joist where it was resting, leaving Barry in darkness. He lost no time in scrambling out but returned to work later, telling himself it was just his imagination. Or was it?

The men later mentioned their experiences to a policeman friend who looked into the history of the house, and discovered that a woman had committed suicide there, by hanging. A possible explanation, but no one will ever know.

There are also stories of a house on the corner of Chalkwell Avenue and Imperial Avenue (now a retirement home) which had a diverse history, ideal for the location of all manner of ghosts. In the 1950s and 1960s it was listed in Kelly's Directory as the 'Southend General Hospital Preliminary Training School and Occupational Therapy Department' but quite conceivably had a war-time role as a convalescent home for wounded soldiers. In the years that it stood derelict (the 1970s), with broken windows and doors hanging from their hinges, it was easy to access by local children – who regretted such visits because of the indefinable fear they experienced once inside (not to mention the abandoned mattresses and old x-rays lying around). This building was opposite Chalkwell Park, with its 'haunted' manor house (*see* page 45).

Denton Avenue

Soon after the Read family moved into their home in 1985, the *Echo* printed a report about a Revd Stanley from St Stephen's Church being called in to bless the dwelling. He had been approached because Mr and Mrs Read had both heard footsteps on the stairs in the dead of night on more than one occasion, when no one else (except their sleeping two-year-old daughter) was in the house. The house, forty years old, had been previously occupied by an elderly couple, and it seems that after his wife had died the husband had committed suicide. The new incumbents had discovered a laurel funeral wreath in the shape of a cross in their garden shed, and felt it appropriate to call in outside intervention – which apparently worked a treat, leaving them, and no doubt the previous occupants, at peace.

Moseley Street

A similar story was once attached to a house here. On this occasion, some time in the 1930s (possibly earlier), the man of the house committed suicide after his wife had left him – by jumping in front of a train on the railway line near Holy Trinity Church. Mrs Hart, who lived here until moving a few doors away just before the Second World War, felt a regular presence, and felt she was being physically pushed and pinched by someone. She also mentioned the word 'poltergeist' when passing this information on to her son, John, so this suggests the sort of activity ascribed to an unfriendly spirit, but it is believed to have ceased when the wife, too, had died.

The Strand (now swallowed up by Southchurch Road)

Sadly demolished in 1958, to make way for a garage and car showroom, was a

A variety of ghostly apparitions. (Image courtesy of www.clipart.com)

large landmark house. It was marked on local maps in the eighteenth century as Tile House (see map on page 20) and was then one of the few substantial houses in the area. Its name was changed in subsequent years to The Oaks and is recorded as part of The Oaks Estate, an impressive plot alongside cornfields, with its own pond and stables. It was then left empty for a number of years. During this period of neglect, a woman's body was found in one of the rooms, long dead.

Older residents in the area claim to have seen the ghost of this unknown woman. Dates have proved difficult to establish, so finding out more about the woman, the finding of the body, or her ghost, has proved as elusive as ectoplasm.

The Strand, incidentally, was less than half a mile west of the White Horse pub in Southchurch Road, and The Oaks was between Chinchilla Road and Surbiton Avenue. The name (Strand) lives on in the nearby Strand Art Gallery.

Southchurch Road

An issue of *Psychic News* dated the 28 January 1956 carried a story about the Woodleys. Richard and his wife Olive lived in a five-roomed part-furnished flat, part of a large three-storey Victorian house – but not for long. Just five weeks after they moved in, Olive heard footsteps on the bare floorboards overhead, which was an empty part of the building.

Then, a few nights later, they were both woken by a loud crash outside their bedroom door. Richard investigated – but found nothing. A few more nights passed in peace, but next they were again woken (at 1 a.m.) by organ music. Richard described the music as 'like somebody playing one

finger exercises' with no tune as such, just 'aimless drawn out notes'. The music was coming from the top floor but the couple did not check it out until the next morning – when they discovered three dust-covered harmoniums that could only be played by operating the foot pedals. They were absolutely astonished, having been totally unaware of the existence of these instruments in the house. Just one more night of this same music and they decided enough was enough – Richard had already taken time off work with the worry.

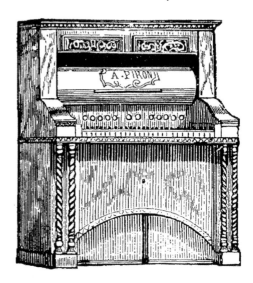

A traditional harmonium, but why did someone abandon three of these beautiful instruments? (Image courtesy of www.clipart.com)

The young couple moved into a friend's home in Shoeburyness, leaving their furniture behind, and were reluctant to go back to retrieve it. A braver friend, Fernando Rossi, who lived in Southend High Street, went to the house with a photographer, in their stead. Both men heard the footsteps that Olive had heard, but they did not hear the music.

There was no follow up to this story in later issues of the *Psychic News*, so the mystery of the harmoniums – who owned them, for instance, and why they were discarded – remains just that, a mystery.

London Road (corner of Electric Avenue)

When Susan Redfern was a young girl in the 1950s she lived on the ground floor of a dwelling that was fronted by a second-hand shop, divided off by a heavy curtain, with another family living above, and a small garden – more of a yard – at the back. This yard was where she would play, ostensibly alone, but was joined regularly by a young girl, a little older and taller, wearing a beret and dated clothes (which would now be described as in the style of the 1930s).

The young girl never spoke, just appeared, but they had their own form of communication – smiles, gestures, signs. When Susan left the yard to enter the house, she waited for her mystery friend to follow her, but at this stage she always disappeared. Her mother listened to her account of these events, but made no comment, nor explanation, and dad was not there to listen to her, as he spent a lot of his time away in the navy.

Towards the end of the last century, Susan and her father and sister re-visited the locale, which was still a shop at the time, and mentioned the cats they always had, one being found frozen stiff on a particularly cold and frosty winter morning. The shopkeeper felt that this explained the smell of cats that still lingered – which even

The modern-day junction of London Road and Electric Avenue. (Author's collection)

a local priest had failed to shift. This corner now has a very different appearance, but does that unknown little girl – and the cats – still visit?

Wakering Road

Long before Eton House School closed in 1993, this beautiful Grade II listed house – once known as Southchurch Lawn and now Alleyn Court Preparatory School – was said to have been haunted by a ghost with a lantern passing by the north frontage. The most likely figure to have a connection with the area is a smuggler, given its proximity to the sea and to the

timing of the earliest manifestations, the 'age of the smuggler'. There were reputedly seventeenth-century tunnels here used by the smuggling fraternity, reaching as far as Porter's (now on the Queensway/Sutton Road roundabout). The school building has an interesting history, having been originally two cottages knocked into one, known locally as 'Bakers and Munns'. It can be seen on eighteenth-century maps as China Hall, named after the lady living there who compared herself to china, while the 'common people' were earthenware!

However, as far as the ghost is concerned, at least one source speculates that this was the ghost of the man who saved the life of Princess Charlotte when she visited

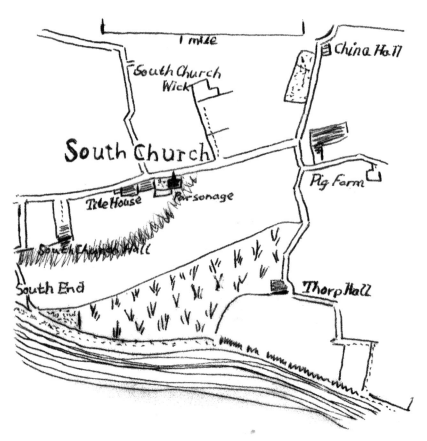

Map of historic Southchurch featuring Tile House (see page 18) and China Hall. (Author's collection)

Southchurch Lawn in around 1801. The man ran out into the road in front of a horse and rider who were bearing down on the princess. This rider, who managed to avoid the royal visitor, was apparently Charles Asplin, and the incident was recorded by his brother Jonas, whose diaries survive in the Essex Record Office. Southchurch Lawn was also reputed to have been visited by Lord Nelson and Lady Hamilton and by Charlotte's parents, Princess Caroline and the Prince Regent. An un-named writer in the *Southend Standard* (25 July 1957) muses romantically of the 'rustle of crinolines and ghost-like strains of a minuet' played for Princess Caroline that could still be heard.

In the same road, on the corner of Elm Road, is a Grade II listed building known as the Red House. This rambling, red-brick house was built in 1673, and is thought to be the servants' quarters of Shoebury Manor, a quarter of a mile away, although the latter was probably built two years later.

During the 1940s, the long-term resident of the Red House, Mrs Phillips, reported, during renovations to the roof, that she had often heard 'knockings and noises'. She revealed that she had tried to trace the sounds, which usually occurred at midnight, by going up and down the stairs, but had never been able to find out the source. The walls were thick enough to persuade her that the sounds definitely came from within the house, rather than outside.

Mrs Phillips' revelations tie in with a much older story of the ghost of a young lady in the same house, a young lady who cut her own throat after a serious disagreement with her lover. It must have been quite a disagreement if she did indeed go to such lengths. As the house also had a secret tunnel connecting it to the original Shoebury Manor, no doubt used by smugglers and perhaps also during the Second World War, then there could be other explanations for the ghost. Nevertheless,

The Red House, Shoeburyness, 100 years ago. (Image courtesy of www.footstepsphotos.co.uk)

Mrs Phillips – who felt that the building was originally an inn, although there seems to be no evidence of this – was more sympathetic to the story of the suicide than other versions.

Leigh Hill

On the front page of the *Southend Pictorial* on the 3 August 1962, there is a photograph of Mrs Vera Smith, JP, on the stairs of her home on Leigh Hill. She had not believed in ghosts until she saw one on the stairs of her eighteenth-century house – which did not have a dark and gloomy interior as you might expect, but was modern, white-walled, light and airy. Early one morning she had seen an elderly, short man with a long coat, knee breeches and stockings on bandy legs with heavy shoes, his hair tied back in a 'cue' (braid). He had hobbled down the stairs, without colour, and with blurred edges, lasting a few seconds before disappearing, and leaving a fishy smell behind him.

Although surprised by what she had seen, it tied in with a young (four-year-old) visitor who had screamed with fear just a few weeks earlier, telling her mother that she had seen a man 'standing in the corner'. They had called round for afternoon tea, and the girl had been unable to describe the figure with any accuracy until some months later when she saw a Toby jug and told her mother that it looked 'just like the man in Prospect House'!

There had been earlier reports of tradesmen who were wary of entering the building because they were convinced it was haunted; such reports date back to 1894. However, when Mrs Smith was approached by a Mr Botting from Boscombe Road, offering to exorcise her ghost, she declined, preferring to leave things as they were. The *Pictorial* mentioned some days later that Mrs Smith, who became the Mayor of Southend from 1969-1970, had also had an enquiry from a demonologist.

A local resident, Wendy Newby, also recalls that next door to Prospect House, a doctor and his housekeeper had lived in the

Leigh Hill, c. 1900. The location of a number of ghosts. (Author's collection)

A typical, but not scary, Toby jug. (Image courtesy of www.clipart.com)

Hauntings (a forerunner of *Ghosts and Hauntings*) of the time she saw a woman in a 'diaphanous dark blue muslin gown which looked old and threadbare' gliding across the landing. When she revealed her experience to someone who had been living in Leigh for many years, the sighting was dismissed as being 'the old lady of Leigh', known to wander around the gardens of Leigh library.

Leighton Avenue

When Wendy Newby was interviewed in 2010, regarding her personal experiences of the paranormal, she had already been living in the same house for over fifty years. During that time, she had a number of experiences, the first being a visit from a chimney sweep in the 1960s, which had resulted in the mysterious disappearance of her husband's pipe rack, which had been on the mantelpiece before the chimney was swept. Neither Mr nor Mrs Newby could trace the pipe rack until after supper when they returned to the room where, hey presto, it was back in the correct position, complete with pipes and no trace of chimney dust. Had someone, or something, been keeping it safe? Had someone, or something, been playing some kind of joke? This has remained a family mystery, with no logical explanation, and sits alongside her grandson's fear of entering one of the bedrooms.

A later experience, after being widowed, was when a friend, who had not known her husband, Jim, saw a man on Wendy's patio holding a pipe by the bowl. This was exactly the way Jim had held his pipe, and the description fitted. This particular experience in part explains why Wendy feels so attached to her home.

early part of the twentieth century, and the housekeeper had inherited the house upon the doctor's death. In what had been the doctor's consulting room, there had been a large table and a tool cabinet, which were still there when the new owner called in some workmen. It seems that when one of the workmen removed a tool from the cabinet for his own use, the table turned upside down in his presence and without explanation. He returned the tool immediately and with some trepidation, and this house, too, acquired a reputation of being haunted by that departed doctor, who objected to anyone else using his tools.

There is another story attached to a different eighteenth-century house also on Leigh Hill, where Joan Ward lived in the 1990s. She wrote in *Essex Ghosts and*

North Street

Although Elaine Bernard remains a sceptic, she has some interesting stories to tell about her home in Leigh-on-Sea. From her bedroom, the daughter of the previous residents could see the Victorian schoolhouse, built at the bottom of the garden along with the original dwelling in 1891. She told her mother – and, latterly, Elaine – that she had seen a tall, thin, severe looking woman with cropped hair moving around in the building, a woman she had found 'scary'. The original residents, who sold the property in 1897, were teachers by the names of Eleanor Howgill, who appears in the 1891 census, and Mary Twycross. The description could easily be one of these two women. It is interesting that they moved into the house, and had the extra construction built, the year after Leigh Board School opened nearby, and rumour has it that they used the 'room' as a music school. Just a few years later, when it was sold, its use had been changed, and housed a tenant instead.

To add to this story, much more recently, a local man had removed some tables from this extra room, which Elaine had used for art work or to entertain her grandchildren – and he told her that he had seen a 'ghost' matching the earlier description who had a message, delivered in a 'school-marmy voice' which effectively 'told' Elaine to make good use of the schoolhouse. Did he know the earlier ghost story? Possibly. Did this influence what he may well have seen? Maybe. Whatever the truth, it remains a fascinating area of conjecture.

The haunted Victorian schoolhouse in the garden in North Street. (Author's Collection)

A Victorian schoolmistress; perhaps she is wondering if she is destined to haunt her workplace for infinity. There are worst places she could do this than Leigh-on-Sea. (Image courtesy of www.clipart.com)

Victor Drive/Grand Drive

On this corner, Peter Fox's father had a second-hand shop in the 1960s. He started off with the downstairs shop and, when the upstairs became vacant, the family moved there. There was plenty of room – living room, bathroom, kitchen and three bedrooms with offices and a store room downstairs – but the years that Peter lived there were memorable for different reasons.

His earliest memories are of the radio in the shop seemingly turning itself on and playing classical music (which no one in Peter's family seemed to appreciate) on more than one occasion. More dramatically, one Saturday in 1963 when his mother and brother were out shopping, and his dad was working in the shop, Peter was in the living room upstairs with the family dog, an Irish wolfhound cross, which suddenly hid behind the chair and started crying. This seems to have been the same day when the clock outside the building started ticking for the first time, although it had no working parts. Peter, then aged eleven, reported both events to his father, who had no explanation for his son, and as a result Peter started having trouble sleeping.

One particular night, having heard unidentifiable sounds when in bed, he decided to sleep in his younger brother's bedroom rather than alone in his own room. He lay awake, facing the wall next to the bed, only to hear the sound of human breathing which didn't come from his brother; screaming, he ran into his parents' bedroom, who were sympathetic, luckily. This did nothing to help him sleep from then on.

These were not the only inexplicable things to happen in this house in the 1960s. Every Wednesday, when they went to the cinema, they shut Peter's pet kitten in the store room. Although the door was locked, with no other exit, the kitten went missing upon their return one Wednesday, and was never found. It was some years later when a woman whose father had owned, and died in, the building called in to the shop. She revealed that her dad had been fond of classical music and that he had hated cats.

Then there was the summer day when his bedroom window was darkened early in the morning by hundreds of bluebottles – the only window in the house so affected. There was also the mysterious red-hot piece of masonry which landed in the kitchen sink one Christmas Day as the family sat down to eat their Christmas dinner.

Needless to say, Peter was keen to move out, and, to his relief, this finally happened, although his dad kept the shop on. However, the Chinese family who moved in to the upstairs accommodation were also bothered by what they described as a 'ghost' although the Fox family had not mentioned their own experiences. This, for Peter, was affirmation that there was a lot more to it than just a vivid imagination.

Peter's father was also convinced that he had seen the ghost of a German officer when clearing out a nearby shop during the same period (1960s). Thia shop also sold second-hand goods and, on one occasion, Peter, who was helping his dad, picked up a German diary among the discarded bric-a-brac. When he showed this to his dad, the response was unexpected, 'Move away from it. He [the German] is standing next to you.' This could well mean that Peter's sensibility may have been inherited.

Ness Road, Shoeburyness

When the Gillies family moved into Royal Engineers' House in 1996, they were the first family to live there for eight years, the house having been empty for four. The name stems from its original purpose as the Royal Engineers' House (allied to other army buildings around and about what was once Shoeburyness Garrison). The building, behind a 16ft metal fence, had a resident ghost, and Julie Gillies told the *Leigh and Westcliff Times* about it retrospectively in 1999.

This figure was a benign chap, who smoked cigars and was no bother – apart from occasionally moving the coal scuttle for reasons of his own. The family christened him 'Colonel' as this was their over-riding impression of him.

This large house, set in over an acre of grounds, had another building which was opened up by local MP Teddy Taylor in 1997 for community services, and the Colonel's appearances became less of a feature of the family's philanthropic life.

Black(e) House (later Leigh House), Leigh-on-Sea

This house, where Broadway West now begins, was demolished in 1927 after 300 years. Philip Benton, the renowned nineteenth-century local historian, wrote that the house was once avoided because it was haunted.

Any ghost here seems to have been active prior to the nineteenth century. When John Loten, the Collector of Customs at Leigh, lived there between 1792 and 1815 he found a human female skeleton under the stairs during renovations. After this gruesome find, which was re-interred in a local churchyard, the ghost no longer troubled the house.

It may well be that the name Black House was derived from the house's mysterious past.

High Street, Leigh-on-Sea, c. 1890 – a hundred years after the hauntings at Black House. (Author's collection)

High Street (Leigh-on-Sea)

When Dr John Cook lived here in the eighteenth century, he was renowned locally for his work as a physician, and included among his acquaintances such luminaries as John Wesley. The doctor was a believer in the supernatural world, and regarded his supernatural visitors as 'benevolent and beneficent spirits' (according to historian Philip Benton).

After Cook's death in 1777, the house, already 100 years old, was closed up because of the rumours of its being haunted, but there was no further activity reported. The initial public alarm may have been influenced by the revelations in Dr Cook's will, with its supposed references to the spirit world. The original will can be inspected – and interpreted – at Essex Record Office.

There was a specific location that was regarded as the place where Dr Cook communed with the supernatural – a room panelled with Spanish mahogany that had a curious 'oratory-like cupboard'. This was uncovered during renovations by Mr Bridge, in 1929, who opened up the old house as Ye Olde Cook's Place (a café). The house has since been demolished, so the panelling and cupboard can no longer be examined.

Glenbervie Drive

In 1956, Pat Gollin and her husband were taken by surprise at the sound of footsteps upstairs. The sound was of bare feet crossing the floor, but no one was up and about. Of course, they double checked, but saw and heard nothing more. However, when a neighbour was babysitting one evening, the sound of footsteps occurred again. This was confirmation for Pat that she hadn't been imagining it.

Out of curiosity, she looked into the history of the house, and found that only one previous family had lived there, from its construction in 1919 to 1950. It transpired that the daughter of this family had died as a young girl, seeming to offer a valid explanation for these experiences.

The house, then and now, has been a happy house full of people and parties, so Pat feels that the little girl was reassured that the new residents were 'worthy' of taking her place.

A Flat in Southend Town Centre

This has proved difficult to locate more specifically, but refers to a story in the then *Evening Echo* in December 1988. The Johnsons were reported to have refused to sleep in their bedroom on the second floor because Joanne Johnson, twenty-five, felt she was being watched. Not only that, but the family dog had a habit of rushing from room to room with raised hackles, there were unexplained cold spots and smells (e.g. of lavender), and objects moving of their own accord.

Things went from bad to worse when their young daughter claimed to have seen 'a man' in their hall, and the shadow of a tall man was seen in their bedroom – added to the sounds of a child playing in another bedroom.

However, this was one occasion when unexplained events and unexplained sights and sounds did not drive the family out. Instead, the flat was blessed by the Revd Keith Dally, then of St John's Church (at the bottom of the High Street), and this seems to have worked a treat.

London Road, Hadleigh

Although the most famous nineteenth-century witch in the area was Cunning Murrell, it is the lesser known Mrs Eves, a rival, who re-appeared after death. Her son was working in a field some distance away when his mother's ghost appeared, prompting him to return to his home, the cottage in London Road they had shared, near the Wagon and Horses (both buildings are now demolished).

The son was afraid that he would inherit his mother's powers, powers he did not want in any shape or form. In front of the two women who had been preparing his mother for burial, he opened a drawer, took out a box that apparently contained 'a live creature' and threw it on the fire. Fearful screams scared the women, but died away as the box and contents turned to ashes.

This astounding story had a happy outcome for the son, at least. The women fled, not surprisingly, but he was heard to say that he was 'free at last' – Mrs Eves having been feared in life as much as in death.

Stambridge Road, Stambridge

Just a mile east of Rochford, this former bakery achieved an element of fame in November 2010 after featuring on Channel 4's *Come Dine With Me*. The hostess, Kelly Tolliday, described as a 'retired police officer' called in psychic medium, Nicky Alan, who also appears on television, to tell her guests about the young boy who haunted her home. Parts of the house date back more than four centuries, so it is a perfect site for such stories.

(Note: Kelly won the £1,000 prize for her menu – which included Canewdon pork!)

A witch with some similarities to Mrs Eves. (Author's collection)

Church Road, Hockley

A family called Murgatroyd moved into the Old School House here in 1957 and, several months later, contacted the Phenomenist Research League regarding their experiences, which were published in the League's journal, *Newscast*.

Prior to coming to the house the family had not had any previous supernatural experiences but several incidents in their new home led them to think quite differently about the world of spiritualism. Since they had moved in, they had found doors open that had been securely closed (using a latch) and bells ringing late at night in the hall.

As the building was a school from 1804 onwards, their thinking was that one of the children was re-visiting her old haunts as a form of poltergeist. They were not afraid or spooked, and instead treated their unseen visitor lightly, christening her Matilda. They expressed the hope that someone or something would actually materialise, which would satisfy their curiosity, but had had no luck up to the time of their account being published.

Lady using a treadle sewing machine, a reminder of days gone by. (Image courtesy of www.clipart.com)

seen an elderly lady sitting at an old treadle machine, busily sewing, in the bedroom at the side of the bungalow.

Although no one else had seen the woman, they could definitely confirm that such a sewing machine had been *in situ*, and some had also experienced a 'presence' in that particular room. This seems to have provided proof to the new tenants that their home was indeed haunted.

Kingsway, on the Hockley/ Hullbridge border

There is a bungalow here that has changed hands on many occasions, but one of the original tenants was an elderly lady with an old-fashioned treadle sewing machine. This machine was left behind for the next family, who painted it so they could use it as a piece of furniture, but did not use it for its original purpose.

Years later, the most recent tenant started asking if anyone who had lived there before her 'knew' that the house was haunted. She was curious as to whether anyone else had

Polly's Farm, on the Hockley/ Hullbridge border

In the 1950s, the Sheppard family lived here, although the farm and its barns have since disappeared with only some concrete flooring and discarded clap-boarding apparent during their last visit some forty years ago.

During their time here, a relative (John), staying for the weekend, was sleeping on the downstairs sofa. The rest of the family who slept upstairs were woken by someone moving about in the downstairs sitting room, someone who was knocking things over. When checking out the noise, they discovered John, shaking, and trying to light a match. It took him a while to calm down, at which point he told them that he had seen the face of an old man looking down at him, a man only a foot or so away. From this point on, other members of the family felt uneasy about staying there – even though this family included macho boxers and squaddies!

The family had heard stories of the farm being haunted, and of how, many years before, some of the local children had tested each other by seeing who could linger at Polly's the longest before getting scared and running out. Kath Sheppard has written of a few incidents that revealed that there was one way the 'house guest' (as she describes the unseen visitor) showed its presence – by opening and closing doors. These doors were not easy to open and close, either, they were the old fashioned type with latches.

Other incidents included a number of occasions when she and her husband, Ron, heard what appeared to be someone falling down the stairs – someone they never saw. Ron also heard what sounded like a harpsichord late one night – he checked out their musical box on the bedroom windowsill in case this was the source of the music, but it played a very different tune and so could not be the cause of the music he had heard.

Their dog, Dandy, a cross Labrador/Alsatian, features in the events at Polly's Farm. There was more than one occasion when he made a lot of fuss, worrying and snarling, until he was let out and could run around outside, barking. This pattern of behaviour stopped as suddenly as it had started.

Even with such disturbances going on, the resident Sheppards never felt threatened or afraid. Perhaps the fact that a) the farm was conceivably a relay station for the earliest stage-coaches, and b) the last stage coach in the area ran nearby (and is said to revisit the area every year) has some relevance. Obviously this is a matter for debate, and a fascinating debate it would be.

(Note: The location is now part of Lords Golf Course.)

Paglesham Church End

In the *Southend Standard* dated 9 September 1943, there was an account of a cottage near Paglesham Church being demolished after a 400-year life span. According to the account, this cottage, constructed with old ship timbers and able to withstand storms coming in from the sea, had attracted 'hundreds of tourists', before the war, because of its haunted status. It seems that even picture postcards were printed and sold – depicting a skeleton at one of the windows of the cottage.

The legend remains a legend, because the last inhabitant, a bargee by the name of Mr Woolf, failed to contact any 'disturbing elements'. The secrets behind its short-lived fame will probably now never be known.

High Street, Canewdon

There is a seventeenth-century cottage here whose current resident has been visited just once by an interesting ghost, although she has lived there for nearly thirty years. The ghost, described as a tall man with a long frock-coat, long grey hair and an impressive grey beard, appeared in the doorway of her dining room one morning in the late 1990s. He was a solid, rather than a ghostly, figure, and prompted an unusual reaction. The lady who lives there told him to 'Sod

Historic Paglesham, site of ancient dwellings, legends – and ghosts. (Author's collection)

Wallasea Island

off!' because she was running late for work. At that, he disappeared – and is perhaps too insulted to have returned.

The only other time this same figure had been seen was in a dream. Although this dream occurred just the night before the man arrived in her doorway, it was certainly not part of the dream (in the dream, he had spoken to a young lad who seemed to be tampering with her car outside the cottage). A psychic has visited the cottage since and confirmed a 'presence'.

Could this be the ghost of George Pickingill, the famous Canewdon witch who matches this description and who exerted his powers until early in the twentieth century? Sybil Webster, a local who has written and researched George Pickingill in impressive detail, has apparently intimated that Pickingill (or whatever variant of his name you care to choose) had actually lived in this very cottage, so …

Because Wallasea Island forms part of the parish of Canewdon, I am taking the liberty of including this more remote part of South Essex – but not that remote, as it is only seven miles from Southend-on-Sea. The story here is particularly fascinating.

This ghost is said to haunt Tile Barn, a farmhouse, known locally as the Devil's House because – in part – of its association with Mother Redcap, a notorious local witch. The name 'Mother Redcap' has been adopted as a generic term for witches, so her real name is unclear – one journalist suggests it was 'Granny Smith' but this seems unlikely, although you never know. (The house was, incidentally, originally called Davill's House after an early, French owner and is on the Chapman and Andre map of 1777 as 'Devil's House'.)

There seems to be little, in this particular case, to separate the terms 'devil' and 'ghost'; both have been, effectively, blamed

An early map incorporating Wallasea Island and Devil's House. (Image courtesy of Peter Owen)

for cattle 'going mad', inducing a sense of 'evil' accompanied by freezing temperatures, and for the sound of flapping wings in empty rooms.

One particular room was avoided by anyone living there, and kept firmly locked until the First World War, when part of the farmhouse was used as a billet. A soldier who stayed in this very room overnight was found sleeping on the floor outside the room the next morning, white-faced, but with no lucid explanation for why he was there.

Another persistent story is of a farm labourer passing the dwelling, who heard someone call his name and entered the empty building. He picked up a length of rope, hearing a voice saying 'Do it! Do it!' and felt the urge to hang himself. Oddly, perhaps, he was apparently saved by a black ape-like creature with gleaming yellow eyes looking down at him – the shock bringing him back to his senses. Well, it would do. It has since been suggested that this creature was (or indeed is) a witch's familiar, albeit an unusual one.

During the Second World War, the farmhouse was bombed – a clear target as one of the few, if not the only, building on the island – and finally washed away in the 1953 floods. Now it is the marshes in the surrounding area that have inherited the ghost of Mother Redcap and her familiar, the former thought to be able to cross the river on a wooden hurdle (rather than by broomstick), without using oars. James Wentworth Day wrote in *Essex Countryside* in April 1968 about this particular witch being seen peeling potatoes at Devil's House, 'nippin' her own lips together and mumbling 'Holly Holly, Brolly Brolly, Redcap, Bonny Bonny.' Catchy!

Victoria Road, Rayleigh

In 1983, Judy Flynn and her family moved into one of two houses built on a plot of land that had once housed an orchard and, latterly, a bungalow called Rosebank. Once they were settled in, Judy often used to smell cigarette smoke when she sat in her lounge by the patio doors, and the smell of lavender was also prevalent. As none of the family smoked, or used lavender, she thought it odd, but did not give it a lot of thought.

That was until, in the 1990s, her daughter, Suzanne, had been watching television in the same room. When she turned to leave the room she saw someone, seated, and looking out of the window. She did not go back into the room immediately, but spoke to her mother about what she had seen: a woman with long black hair, not elderly, wearing a vintage ankle-length white dress. This was a hazy, but very obvious, image, no longer in evidence when the two women returned to the room. In the meantime, both Judy and Suzanne had admitted to hearing footsteps upstairs when the rooms were empty, and to seeing a door opening and hearing someone entering, the door closing behind them – even the dog had been puzzled by the latter event because no one could be seen.

As a result of their experiences, they asked their neighbour about the history of the site, before the houses were built. It transpired that the bungalow had been built at the turn of the century, and a long-term female resident had died there in 1972, having spent her final years there. The bungalow and its extensive gardens had apparently given her great pleasure, and she had enjoyed sitting in her scullery (where the Flynn's lounge is now located) smoking and looking out of the window.

The original Rosebank – gone, but still visited. (Image courtesy of Judy Flynn)

For Judy and her family, this was explanation enough. They felt that the old lady had been sad to see what had happened to her former home, and was re-visiting. She was a benevolent visitor, and had something in common with Suzanne: her long dark hair. In fact, whenever Suzanne's hairbrush goes missing for a few days, she wonders if it has been 'borrowed' by her spectral visitor – who also seemed to take a liking to Suzanne's hair-clips which were often moved around. This same hairbrush has even ended up on her pillow – not somewhere she would have left it.

Although Suzanne's sighting in the lounge was the only time this woman has been seen, the sounds and smells continue to this day – and have been witnessed by other members of the family and by the dog of course.

Victoria Avenue, Prittlewell

Recently Leigh Lacey-Marques moved into a house, one of Southend's oldest that dates back to the 1400s, and since then she has felt a lot of energy in the building. Although Leigh regards herself as a 'sensitive', she has not been the only one to feel someone touching her and stroking her hair – husband, friends and family have already had similar experiences on a regular (almost daily) basis.

On one occasion, Leigh thought her husband was running his fingers through her hair after they had gone to bed, but she turned to find he was facing in the opposite direction – fast asleep. The two of them shared the experience of being woken during the night by the sound of a child speaking within the room.

Leigh is currently researching her house, and the result of her search should make interesting reading. Hopefully the story will prove to be a happy one.

(Note: Leigh is one of those behind the setting up of s-o-s paranormal.)

HISTORIC BUILDINGS

These are the buildings that are perhaps more predictably haunted. They have been around for a long time, and been lived in by multiple generations. Those that remain are featured in local guidebooks, although their ghosts do not usually feature.

Rochford Hall

Originally a very large sixteenth-century home (with some twelfth and thirteenth-century origins), Rochford Hall started life as an impressive red-brick building, one of the largest in Essex, with a number of courtyards and walls over 2ft 6in thick. Some of its Tudor architecture remains to be seen on the Rochford Hundred golf clubhouse, the last vestige of the original Hall.

The Hall's most famous residents were the Boleyn family. It was inherited in 1515 by Thomas Boleyn, father of Anne and Mary, with their notorious connections to Henry VIII. Anne is popularly believed to have spent some of her childhood at the Hall, and, later, to have met up from here with the King when he visited Rochford Park on hunting expeditions. Mary, her older sister, settled at Rochford Hall after Anne's death, and died there in 1543, but it is Anne, not Mary, who is reputed to haunt the location.

A particularly colourful, if gruesome, story relates to Anne's execution in 1536 at the Tower of London. The walls and floor of the nursery she had slept in at the Hall were said to run red with blood when news of her death reached Rochford. This, indeed, became a bit of a tourist attraction at the beginning of the twentieth century when the wife of the then tenant-farmer showed people this room as a rather lucrative sideline, charging around 3d per person. The red stains on the floor at the time were, however, dismissed as vestiges of red ink to substantiate the myth! Accounts of the haunting of this room were still being reported as recently as 1928 but the room's exact location is now difficult to pinpoint.

The renovated remains of Rochford Hall, now the golf clubhouse. (Author's Collection)

After years of decay at the Hall (following a fire), a letter dated August 1776 from the Revd Nicholas Griffinhoofe, the rector of Woodham Mortimer, is the earliest written record of paranormal activity here. The letter has often been quoted by local historians. He asserted that the 'Rochford Hall ghost' was growing ruder by the day, throwing boots and shoes at men's heads, although this does not seem to be a reference to Anne Boleyn as he refers to the ghost as 'he'. In September of the same year, the rector writes of the ghost still 'molesting' local folk, but he had personally been unable to exorcise the ghost due to previous commitments. Revd Griffinhoofe was probably peeved by this as he seems to have shown more interest than those clerics located much closer to Rochford (several miles to the South of Woodham Mortimer); certainly no other written reports of this nature have yet been unearthed. There is a passing reference by George Savill towards the end of the nineteenth century. George, a nephew of the owner (James Tabor), lived in what was then a dilapidated mansion, and described his residence as 'rat, if not ghost, haunted'.

Although Anne did not die at Rochford Hall, there is a legend that her heart was carried there and remained for one night before being taken to East Horndon for burial … a heart motif was used as a decorative feature on one wall, but whether this has any connection is difficult to ascertain.

It is still said that a frightening spirit in white and/or a headless woman dressed in silks is a regular sight to be seen in the grounds of what was once the magnificent Rochford Hall. Some locals regard such manifestations as those of witches, and Anne is remembered to have had an aversion to church bells – in common with witches of the period. So is the headless woman Anne, or a local witch? Surely Anne is more likely, as she died at the end of the executioner's sword, not the usual fate for witches. As for the unidentified spirit in white, the twelve nights after Christmas are the most popular times for this sighting – and even poachers were said to avoid the Hall at that time. It certainly seems a good ploy to deter the criminal element! (Interestingly, her sister, Mary, the 'other' Boleyn girl, who died at Rochford Hall, is not mentioned in this context.)

Although Anne Boleyn's ghost is also said to haunt the Tower of London – the location of her execution – as well as Blickling Hall in Norfolk, Anne's birthplace, and Hever Castle in Kent, Anne's childhood home, this does not mean she could not also haunt Rochford Hall. Why should a ghost be restricted to one place? It hardly seems to make full use of the resources available to such immortal beings.

Hadleigh Castle

At the time of Dick Turpin and his Essex gang in the eighteenth century, the castle, with its fine views of the Thames, Southend and Leigh-on-Sea, had already been in ruins for some 200 years. It was renowned as a place to be avoided because of the ghosts that haunted it. Certainly, there were reports of lights flickering on and off, of shadows and mysterious sounds, but these can easily be attributed to smugglers, wanting to keep the hoi polloi – and the Customs officers – at arm's length.

One story that is less easy to explain away, however, is that of a milkmaid from nearby Castle Farm who saw a woman in white early one morning, and obeyed her 'instructions' to meet her at the castle at midnight, when the woman would reveal some of the ruin's mysteries. The maid was too frightened to attend but, unluckily, met the vision again by chance the next morning and was apparently cuffed over the ear because she had broken her word – a vision obviously with some strength because it seems the girl's neck was almost dislocated. As a result, this milkmaid was thereafter known as Wry-neck Sal, with her head permanently misaligned to one side. Castle Farm, incidentally, dates from the early eighteenth century, and was demolished in the 1970s.

According to another source, this white lady was said to have made dramatic appearances just before a shipment of illicit liquor arrived, promptly disappearing when the haul had been moved away from the castle. So perhaps Wry-neck Sal had a more likely explanation for her disability, one she did not wish to reveal … or perhaps not.

Eric Maple tells (in *The Realm of Ghosts*) of a rather different but still 'mysterious White Lady.' His research refers to a lady wandering at night offering to dance with anyone, male or female, who passed that way. It seems that if she wearied of a dancing partner, however, she would hurl them over the walls of the castle into the dried up moat below. Assuming that this is the same mystery woman, could Wry-neck Sal have been one of her dancing victims? This par-

HADLEIGH CASTLE, *in* ESSEX.

The ancient ruins of Hadleigh Castle. (Richard Platt collection)

ticular author also refers to a 'Black Man' lurking in the shadows who would purchase a soul for a song. Go back far enough in folklore and here you have the devil and the female spirit of the river.

Reports of a phantom dog (Black Shuck), and even a monk, continue from time to time, and the setting has attracted public ghost hunts in recent years.

The original castle dates back to the thirteenth century, and, although the remaining towers are a prominent feature seen from the Thames Estuary, it is largely concealed from nearby residents by more modern developments. It is certainly not that easy to locate or approach as the fields below the ruins are made inaccessible by the railway line – its remoteness making it an ideal situation for paranormal activity.

What will the mountain bikers in the 2012 Olympics make of the castle – and the white lady – when cycling around its perimeters?

Prittlewell Priory

The priory, founded in around 1110 as a self-contained community for Cluniac Benedictine monks and now a museum, was not always a place of peace and reflection. For example, in 1321, the Prior of Lewes decided to take control from Prior William by force, resulting in what seems to have been a bloody battle, with Prior William fatally injured. Could William be the monk whose ghost is said to haunt the Priory building and surrounding park? An archaeological dig in the grounds in the 1960s revealed the burial of a monk (supposedly) following an ancient tradition that showed he had been disgraced, i.e. the head had been removed from the body and placed face down – facing Hell.

A more romantic notion, perhaps, is of a later monk falling in love with a local girl, both of whom disappeared after their secret was discovered by monastic authorities.

An unexplained orb more recently seen at Hadleigh Castle. (Image courtesy of Mr Burpy at www.flickr.com)

A peaceful twenty-first century Prittlewell Priory. (Author's Collection)

As a result, rumours circulated that the monk had been put to death and the girl had been imprisoned in the priory. Could this lovelorn monk have been the one buried in disgrace? Did he perhaps practice black magic, as has been suggested? What happened to the girl?

An area once used as the minstrel's gallery seems to have been a favoured spot for a ghostly monk to appear. The gallery was also the location for the sound of children playing. In 1987, they were heard – unusually – by two people, the museum's supervisor and attendant. The two men investigated what sounded like laughter but the gallery, or balcony, was deserted. Nevertheless, both men were convinced that the sounds related to the ghosts of children. It is reasonable to surmise that the children could have been members of the Scratton family who lived in the priory

between the seventeenth and twentieth centuries and themselves wrote ghost stories in their diaries. This particular sighting was reported in the local *Evening Echo* with an additional reference to a ghostly monk seen on the path leading from the original cloisters to the church. The museum supervisor was obviously a person receptive to the spirit world, because he had a further personal experience when he saw a figure of a white-shirted man walking from the garden towards the refectory and who disappeared before reaching the door.

Another mystery figure was spotted in a photograph taken in Priory Park by a photographic student from Southend College. The photo showed the intended girl on a park bench, but accompanied by an additional dark shape bending over her, which could be identified only as a shrouded figure. No explanation was ever found for

The interior of Prittlewell Priory – site of so many 'stories'. (Author's collection)

drowning) has been difficult to pin down.

Yet another ghost story attributed to the grounds of Prittlewell Priory is detailed by Wes Downes in issue no. 15 of *Ghosts and Hauntings*. Since it became privately owned (i.e. since the sixteenth century), it seems that another legend has grown apace. This version tells of one of the former owners who is said to have cut his own throat so badly that he nearly severed his head. His semi-decapitated figure is another ghostly apparition said to roam the grounds – and could also of course be the origin of the decapitated skeleton.

Very close to the priory, in Priory Crescent, is an industrial area said to have been the site of the original burial ground for the priory. The buildings here have been demolished in recent years, but one building that was home to local business E.K. Cole (EKCO Radio) and, latterly, the Royal Bank of Scotland (Access House), acquired a reputation for being haunted. Security guards recorded seeing 'black figures' in twentieth-century offices, and there was an incident of a chair gliding across the room with no explanation, and lifts going up and down when not in use. Given its history and location, these sightings have to be linked, surely.

No ghosts have yet been linked to the finding of the grave of the seventh-century (Saxon) Prince of Prittlewell on the park's perimeter in 2003. However, there is a

this anomaly, or for a late-night chorus of 'Onward Christian Soldiers' heard in the park and reported by a local in recent years.

There are also a number of claims that a ghost has been seen by the pond in the extensive grounds that now form Priory Park. In the middle of the pond is a small island known as Duck Island, for obvious reasons, and it is the squawking of these wildfowl that is said to herald the presence of a monk. The pond is, additionally, linked to the ghost of a bride who is supposed to have drowned there, but this event (the

Ghostly monks, often associated with Prittlewell Priory and its grounds. (Image courtesy of www.clipart.com)

poem, 'History Beneath the Arcades', by D.S. Davidson, which includes the lines:

> There's a haunted fort of Roman or
>   Celtic vintage
> And buried Princes below Prittlewell
> Now time keeps them all secreted well.

There is plenty of material here for ongoing speculation, research and debate for many years to come. The priory itself, incidentally, is in the throes of a twenty-first-century re-vamp, which may put an end to these sightings ... or maybe not.

Lapwater Hall

In 1751, this impressive building with its surrounding 125 acres – which once featured on the maps of Leigh-on-Sea – was totally renovated as the residence of one Gilbert Craddock (financier by day, and a highwayman using the name Cutter Lynch by night). However, the house, formerly Leigh Park House, is long gone.

It seems that the workmen and journeymen responsible for the construction of the house were used to a minimum of two pots of ale a day as a part of their wage, with occasionally more. When the mean Gilbert Craddock broke with this tradition, the Essex men were not best pleased at being deprived of their Essex beer. His response to their complaints was that they should 'go to the pond and lap water'.

It is unlikely that these workers therefore shed many a tear when Craddock ended up dead in this very pond, soon after his country seat had been completed. He had drowned after being shot at late one night by the Bow Street Runners, who were determined to 'get their man' – whether suicide or accident is debatable.

One of these workers was Amos Tricker, and one of Amos's tasks had been to fill Craddock's wine cellar with a large quantity of ale, wine and brandy. So when 'Nan Tricker' (his daughter) got married some months after Craddock's burial, Amos – who knew the location of the keys to the now empty Lapwater Hall (so named by the workers for obvious reasons) – decided he had every right to help himself.

However, he only got as far as the cellar steps when he saw a squint-eyed figure with the ugly face of a bulldog, none other than Gilbert Craddock, or Cutter Lynch. Amos, who claimed to have been the first person to set eyes on Gilbert Craddock when he first arrived to view Leigh Park House in January 1751, was now the first to see his ghost. Craddock, or Lynch, had a mug in his hand, and beckoned Amos to drink his fill. Not surprisingly, Amos turned and ran instead. This figure, offering ale – which

was said to be some form of redemption for the insult he had inflicted – was then seen by others who subsequently ventured into the cellars, but it seems no one accepted the offer of a drink. If they had, would the ghost have then disappeared, duly appeased?

Interestingly, the same figure was once said to haunt the old pump that existed in the grounds, cranking the handle and still saying 'let them lap water'. To show how such stories evolve, however, look no further than Jessie Payne's father who heard tell of an instrument of torture in the cellar of Lapwater Hall, which turned out to be an old cheese press.

The Hall was demolished in 1947, but the name Lapwater lives on in Lapwater Close. At some stage, perhaps during the development of Lapwater Close, the cellars were filled in. This, finally, seems to have seen the end of the ghost of this once disreputable figure, who had two sides to his nature: on the one hand, he was an educated chess player, engaged to Lady Eleanor of Eden House (or Eden Lodge), but on the

Lapwater Hall by Tony Pitt-Stanley, from Legends of Leigh, *by Sheila Pitt-Stanley. (Image courtesy of Ian Wilkes)*

Ghostly representation of a legendary highwayman.
(Image courtesy of Toby Williams)

other, he was known to lash out with his riding whip if anyone upset him at the local pub, The Smack.

His horse, incidentally, Brown Meg, was just as famous for a while – the horse had no ears, and Cutter Lynch, the highwayman, had wax replicas made so that Brown Meg could not be identified by the law!

Old House, Rochford

This Grade I listed building in South Street, owned by Rochford Council and dating back to 1270, can claim to be the most haunted house in the area. We are not just talking one ghost – we're talking a good half dozen.

One worker, in 1984, had the courage to spend a night here to check out stories she was hearing from builders and restorers who had been working on the house. Joined by five other interested parties (including a medium), their investigations were published in the *Evening Echo* on the 3 October. Not surprisingly, it was the medium who had the most to report – a woman's screams,

an Edwardian child apparently looking for her mother, a Puritan woman surrounded by children, a maid carrying a tray, a strong man in a green medieval costume, a laughing Victorian girl in a white dress, plus other less detailed shadowy figures. Jacqueline English, the employee, started out as a sceptic, but had all her fears confirmed.

Two years later, the *Evening Echo* printed further confirmation of the building's haunted status. It seems that the cleaners who worked at night would only work in twos because, individually, they had witnessed lights on in what should have been darkened rooms, and several had seen a figure of a man sitting in a chair in the office of the Chief Executive. Some cleaners had even left their job because of what they had witnessed.

The Chief Executive himself, Arthur Cooke, also had a strange tale to tell. He had shown a visitor – Sandra Berry – into his office, who was immediately overwhelmed by the atmosphere in the room, and who told him she could see a man sitting in the corner by the fireplace. She was able to describe the man as elderly, with a dark grey salt and pepper beard and long moustache, wearing a black waistcoat. The apparition swiftly disappeared, leaving Mrs Berry with the hairs standing up on her arms – although the atmosphere was not apparently unpleasant, it was more a feeling of benevolence. This certainly seems to have been the same man seen by the cleaners, and also 'sensed' by Mr Cooke's secretary, Eve Bakewell.

Identifying this particular ghost has been impossible, partly because of the number of people who have lived – and even died – in the house in its 700-year history. The *Echo*, however, did print a picture of the haunted chair in question, complete with what could easily be construed as a 'ghost'.

Chalkwell Hall

There was a letter from an 'A.B. Osborne' in the February/March 1958 issue of *Essex Countryside* which offered a more logical explanation of the ghost ('a white shape') that had been seen here on occasion. The Hall was a place which Leigh fishermen were reputed to steer clear of after dark. At the time, Chalkwell Hall was approached via a wide white gate and lengthy drive. One night, Mr Osborne was walking past the entrance gate after missing the last train from Southend to Leigh-on-Sea, following a visit to the theatre.

It was apparently a wild night, with plenty of cloud and a small moon occasionally visible, but a pleasant walk with no traffic and few passers-by. Under the belt of trees that lined the road at this point, it was extra dark, and he could hear the sound of muffled footsteps which seemed to be getting nearer, approaching him from the drive. Feeling brave, he walked right up to the gate and listened, catching a glimpse of a white shroud which was not close enough to make out clearly. Suddenly, however, the moon shone through the clouds, the clock struck twelve, and ... an old white horse put his head over the gate and neighed.

Was this indeed the real explanation for the 'ghost' of Chalkwell Hall? Would the stalwart Leigh fishermen have been fooled so easily?

Shoeburyness Garrison

Early in the nineteenth century, the Shoebury area, east of Southend, became an army garrison town, and set up a school of gunnery with artillery ranges. But it

Chalkwell Hall as it looks now, in the centre of Chalkwell Park. (Author's Collection)

had been of strategic importance since prehistoric times, and has a wonderful setting on the edge of the Thames Estuary with adjacent nature reserves. The remaining buildings are slowly being turned into 'luxury' housing, with a number of listed buildings among them – the gunnery drill shed for example.

During the world wars of the twentieth century, the garrison played a vital role in the defence of Southend, and as an experimental area for a range of weapons. As a result of its sometimes rather bloody history, and of the sheer volume of troops and others that have lived here, it is not surprising that this history also incorporates a number of ghostly happenings.

The barracks area inhabited by the WRAC during the Second World War is reputed to be haunted by the ghosts of several of those killed during a fire at this location. Not far away, a young Wendy Newby was billeted for a while in the Nissen huts in Wakering Road with her sister, close to an ammunition dump. This uncomfortable billet was

soon upgraded to the end house of a block in the garrison itself, although there was only a bed and a locker in the way of furnishing in Wendy's quarters.

The first suggestion that Wendy had of anything untoward was when her friend Peggy, another ATS girl who worked on the ranges (Wendy was in the offices), announced that she could see a face other than her own in every mirror in the house. This was obviously something that was not only worrying her, but was also un-nerving for the other girls.

Wendy shared her small room half way up the staircase with two others, and is convinced that during one dark night she felt a hot breath on her cheek and on the back of her hand, breathing that she could clearly hear, but with no one else awake in the room. This scared her so much that, aged eighteen, she needed comforting by one of the older girls.

Another rather odd incident was when the girls set up a booby trap for the 'last one in' over the door to the upstairs quarters.

The entrance to Shoebury Garrison, before its late-twentieth-century redevelopment. (Author's collection)

The poker and the coal tongs that they had put in place, which should have made a loud clatter when the stiff door was opened, were on the floor as expected the next morning, but not a sound had been heard. While this could have several explanations, Wendy has dismissed them, and the fact that she still remembers the incident to this day speaks volumes. At the time, she refused to sleep in that particular house again.

As the Messing Clerk for the whole garrison (except the officers' mess), Wendy worked from a small desk in the men's administrative offices, and felt she should tell someone of her experiences. A young officer overheard her repeating these events, and agreed that he 'knew' that the house was haunted – resulting in all the girls moving out the same day to another block. Wendy lives just a few miles away now, in Leigh-on-Sea, and has returned to try and locate the haunted building she remembers. However, the re-development has been on such a grand scale that she has found this impossible.

Southend Pier

It has proved difficult to pin down the stories attributed to the town's historic pier, still the longest pleasure pier in the world. The end of the pier, near to the RNLI lifeboat house and shop, has been the subject of a number of sightings after dark. One particular tall 'man with a long coat' was chased in a late autumn evening in 1992 by a policeman but disappeared at the far end, where there is a sheer drop into the Thames – an event recorded on a number of websites, although all reports are second-hand. One first-hand report, however, is on the Essex Paranormal website, where a contributor has seen a figure under the pier 'on many occasions' and has also experienced the 'feeling' of a man actually hanging underneath the structure.

At the other end of the pier, where it meets a row of small restaurants and shops below Pier Hill, there used to be a flight of steps, demolished during the modernisation of the pier's entrance in 2004. During

Glimpse of Shoebury Barracks more than fifty years ago, hiding its secrets. (Author's collection)

the renovations, there were reports of a woman in black, supposedly trying to climb these stairs; a spectre which appears to have resulted in a workman running from the scene 'in terror'.

As the very first – and very different – pier was first constructed in 1830, such stories have had time to mature, and come as no surprise. There have been a number of cases of people committing suicide by jumping from the end of the pier over the years, which adds to its 'suitability' for tales of things that go bump, or splash, in the night.

MORE HISTORIC BUILDINGS

There are a few additional historic locations in Southend which seem to be the ideal setting for visits from past inhabitants: particularly the fourteenth-century Southchurch Hall, now a museum, and the fifteenth-/sixteenth-century Porters – the Civic House and Mayor's Parlour. However, although there are occasional references to ghosts in these locations over the years, such stories have all been vague (mainly mysterious footsteps), and quite probably fictionalised. Even Southend Museum, originally Southend Library, which only dates back to 1905, offers a story of a ghost of a young girl dressed in yellow for visitors at dusk who are susceptible to an awareness of all things strange or spooky.

ENTERTAINMENT VENUES

The following locations have turned out to be a particularly fruitful source of unexplained and paranormal experiences, or 'all things strange and spooky'. So many people have worked in these locations over the years, and so many thousands have visited them, it is not surprising that an array of spirits and spectres have been left behind.

SOUTHEND PIER — LONGEST IN THE WORLD   Photograph by Hubert Thompson, A.R.P.S.

Mid-twentieth-century photograph of Southend Pier – still the longest (pleasure) pier in the world. (Author's collection)

Empire Theatre, Alexandra Street

Currently, this is a very unprepossessing building, solidly red brick, utilitarian, and tightly sealed against intruders – although it was described in its early years as 'the prettiest theatre outside London'. For passers-by, little remains of its past glories as a theatre (The Alexandra before becoming the Empire) and as a cinema (The Rivoli/The ABC /The Cannon). But its bland exterior hides a few ghostly secrets.

In a 1987 issue of the local *Yellow Advertiser* (18 March) the then manager of the Cannon cinema, Dean Wren, admitted that he was initially sceptical on commencing his appointment a couple of years earlier, ignoring tales he had heard from former members of staff. These tales told of George, a man who seemingly jumped off the roof when the building was a music hall, but who had returned on numerous occasions to cause harmless mischief.

Mr Wren's understanding was that ghostly George's 'base' was a completely sealed room between the ceiling of the cinema and the roof. Although anyone solid could walk around the room, there was no way in for them – but this was not a problem for George. The manager's own experiences encompassed lights being switched off behind him when he was alone, and the sight of the massive, heavy chandeliers rocking backwards and forwards with no human hand on site, or physically able, to guide them. He also had a particularly odd experience after putting wage envelopes in the safe, in that on his return to open them they had all been reversed; and he had been converted to a belief in the hereafter by such incidents.

The early morning cleaners, working at twilight, had spotted the resident ghost on a number of occasions, standing at the back of the stalls, whistling. Other former members of staff recount numerous sightings of shadowy figures, and a former manager had called the police at one time because of a lot of unexplained noise in the empty building – but no one had been found, and he, too, had decided that it was George, making more noise than usual.

BBC Essex made a series of radio broadcasts around the same time, featuring 'ghost theatres' and their expert regarded the venue as particularly promising because there was an old theatre at its heart with a modern cinema built above. Mystery passages, gloomy stairways and underground cellars all add to the promise for those interested in the paranormal – but there have never been sightings during performances, so the paying public would have been unaware of what was going on behind the scenes.

There are other stories attached to The 'New' Empire (its most recent identity). When the Victorian building, originally a public hall, was gutted by fire after a pantomime performance in January 1895, there were rumours that a homeless person was burned to death. In 1896, after the cinema was re-built, its then owner was rumoured to have thrown himself off the top of the theatre, following bankruptcy; but there appears to be a lot of dramatic Victorian embroidery attached to this particular story. Recent research has revealed that the owner (Fred Marlow) avoided both bankruptcy and suicide! There have been similar unfounded rumours of 'another' suicide when a senior member of staff threw himself from the roof impaling himself on iron bars below, again pre-twentieth century. Was this George, or another?

Such is its reputation that ghost hunts have been organised here by such organisations as Psychic Nights and Spooky

Empire Theatre, c. 1908; its current façade now very different indeed. (Image courtesy of Lynn Tait)

Locations, and, while attendees have been apparently delighted with what they saw, felt and heard, their individual stories are strictly under wraps.

The Kursaal

Bill Raymond told me about the time he was working on night security at this iconic Southend landmark in the 1990s. He recalls expecting a new cleaning lady one morning, due to arrive an hour later than the others (about a dozen in all), i.e. at around 7 a.m., but she had not shown up by 7.30 a.m. Bill started making the cleaning staff their regular morning cuppa during their break when he was hailed by one of the few male cleaners (the majority were women) who announced that the 'new lady' was waiting in the main bar. 'What do you want me to do?' he asked Bill.

Bill Raymond.

Bill was baffled by this unexpected arrival as all the doors of the building were locked, no one had been spotted on the security camera, and no one had knocked to gain entry. The man described her as wearing 'a green coat' and the two men returned to the bar to see how she had managed to gain entry – but there was no sight of her. Bill wondered if the male cleaner had been helping himself to a drink from behind the bar, which he denied vehemently, and then the two of them heard the sound of the lift outside in the foyer. They went to check out who had gone upstairs but there was no-one on the upper floor, although the lift had arrived on this floor, so someone had seemingly sent it up, or …

A still mystified Bill mentioned the incident to another of the cleaners. She had some experience of the spirit world, and was convinced that the woman who had disappeared had been working at the Kursaal in the days before it had been refurbished, before the lift had been installed, and had walked 'through' the lift to the passage that used to be there, which led to the outside amusements. The green coat, and the green scarf or hairnet which

The disappearing cleaner.
(Image courtesy of Toby Williams)

had also been identified, could well have meant that this woman had also been a cleaner – but before the war. This particular lady assured Bill that there were dozens of people around him that he couldn't see, and she had a romantic notion that some of the

Southend's legendary Kursaal in its heyday. (Image courtesy of www.footstepsphotos.co.uk)

men who had died during the war could have returned to the building to find the women they had danced with during the Kursaal's heyday as a dance hall.

This was not Bill's only experience by any means. One of his solitary duties (before the cleaning team arrived) was to walk around the building regularly, and he is absolutely sure that he heard footsteps following behind him when on the upper floor, which he felt sure belonged to a man rather than a woman. He also checked out the ground-floor bowling alley as part of his duties, and, one early morning when entering this area, the sound system started up, again with no-one else in the building. There were other incidents, too, of lights coming on in this area when he was alone.

There is one more tale that Bill had to relate about the Kursaal, but this one is hearsay. Yet another of the cleaning army that tackled this large space had sought him out after an experience that had left her in tears, or, to quote Bill, 'in a terrible state'. He made her a cup of tea and listened to her story. When cleaning one of the one-arm bandits in the foyer a voice shouted out 'Leave me alone!' several times. As she was alone in the area, this had really frightened her, and, from then on, she avoided the machines, leaving this task to someone else.

Interestingly, these accounts tie in with those of Wendy Pullman, a Romany and clairvoyant, who was also part of the 1990s' cleaning team at the Kursaal. Wendy had seen a solid – rather than transparent – figure of a woman in her 50s, wearing some kind of overall/uniform, when she was working in the café at the end of the twenty-lane bowling alley. The figure had disappeared from sight after a few minutes. Wendy had 'felt' someone 'many other times' when cleaning, and had heard a female voice along with music dating from the Second

World War and the rattling of plates in the kitchen when it was empty – sounds that no one else had heard but which could not have been mistaken for anything else.

Additionally, when walking past the café kitchen oven, she had seen a moving shape at the same time as a dramatic drop in the temperature, and this cold feeling had re-visited her on other occasions. Other unexplained events during Wendy's time at the venue included beer mats falling off tables of their own accord – even the vacuum cleaner turning itself off. It seems she had some sort of experience just about every day she worked there, but she never felt threatened, and her feeling is that these were women (men do not seem to feature) returning to where they were happiest, dancing with loved ones before the Second World War. While the notion could be dismissed as romantic, ghosts and spirits often have romantic associations as well as grim ones.

It is not at all surprising that this particular building should offer a handsome supply of ghosts, as so many visitors have been through its portals since it was built in 1901. The 26-acre amusement park once at the rear is long gone as is the famous Wall of Death, the ballroom, and the indoor side shows. The splendid dome remains, with the bowling alley still open at the time of writing, but some of the first-floor function rooms are disused and eerily empty.

The Cliffs Pavilion, Station Road

Built on the site of a large house once owned by Southend's mayor (Frederick Ramuz), this is an unlikely modern structure (1964) to boast of a ghost. However, the stories here are a little unusual in that they pre-date the major 1991 overhaul, i.e. such renovation work would have been more likely to unearth the unexpected. Bar staff before 1991 had inherited a tale of a man dying on site during the 1960s build, and this poor soul (if the story is true) was given the blame when the glass jugs were seen swinging in the Maritime Room on the lower floor, even though doors and windows were all shut. This it seems was a frequent event.

Apart from this, staff working back stage told of unexplained noises under the stage and a nasty chill in the same area, so Emma Bearman, an ex-employee, decided to see if her aunt, who was sensitive to such atmospheres, could shed any light. The result was her aunt's conviction that a death had indeed occurred during the build – and her summarising of the situation was that he would like to leave but was unable to do so. As there have been ongoing substantial renovations since then, perhaps he has managed to make his escape as there are no recent repeats of these events of twenty years ago.

The Palace Theatre, London Road

Ron Wordley's grandfather, Jim, died in February 1929 shortly after falling from the flies of this theatre. He had spent twenty years building and working for The Palace, which opened in 1912. He started working on the construction of the theatre as a scaffolder, but was then employed as a general handyman until his death. The theatre certainly played a pivotal role in Jim's life – he would take home visiting actors who could not find lodgings, or even chorus girls – proving what a very special wife he had! She managed such hospitality despite having eight children living in their home in nearby Fairfax Drive, some of whom

also worked at The Palace – as dressers or 'extras'.

The Wordley family are very aware of the ghost stories attached to the theatre, and they are convinced that if there is such a spirit, that spirit is Jim, and that The Palace could have no finer guardian angel.

However, non-Wordleys tell a different story. Their tale is of George, a former manager who committed suicide by hanging himself from the fly-floor after getting into financial difficulties in 1912; obviously a popular name in theatrical circles (see The Empire's ghost). Sightings of George – or Jim – have been accompanied by the smell of Old Holborn tobacco, and some theatre-goers have felt a hand on their shoulder when the seat beside them was unoccupied. Add to this the sound of an unearthly piano, and the theatre's reputation becomes easier to understand.

Societies such as Clear Sight, Aspire, and North Essex Ghost Hunters have camped out in the building at different times, to look into its spiritual history since the start of the twenty-first century. They have used high-tech equipment as well as mediums and spiritualists, and have uncovered a whole host of ethereal residents as well as unexplained orbs of light, smells (e.g. of tobacco, talcum powder, garlic) and sounds – tapping, knocking, clicking. Different parts of the building – dressing rooms, the dress circle, under the stage, performance spaces – were checked out individually, with activity, smells, sounds, all recorded in comprehensive detail. Here are just a few of the fascinating 'sightings' that took place in the auditorium, staff rooms, under the stage and in the upstairs Dixon Studio during investigations:

- The sight of a cross 5ft high, on fire
- Someone calling out the names of the apostles

Jim Wordley, right, working on the Palace Theatre pre-1912. (Image courtesy of Ron Wordley)

- A clergyman, Victorian style, whose name appears to be Ebenezer
- A young Irish woman from around 1900, probably working as a dresser
- The sense of a child falling from the circle
- A young woman in a red evening gown, singing on the stage

The evidence that these organisations have unearthed would seem to qualify the Palace Theatre as one of the most haunted location in the Southend area. Pinning down the origins of these ghosts, however, is much more difficult. Perhaps someone out there will investigate further, and reach a more finite conclusion.

Jim Wordley, back left, and Jim's son, back right, with Palace Theatre staff. (Image courtesy of Ron Wordley)

two

Haunted Churches and Rectories

Sutton Rectory, Sutton Road

Less than a mile from Southend Airport, the rectory here offered a very long-standing ghost. Sightings date back to its origins in the seventeenth century, the early reports describing a very traditional manifestation in clanking chains. Over the years, successive rectors have reported on 'ghostly' sounds and shadows.

More recently, in the twentieth century, Revd Williams (in the 1930s) saw a figure, dressed in dark clothing similar to a monk, but completely transparent, walking down the stairs of the rectory and into the dining room – not just once, but on several occasions. His wife heard what appears to have been the same apparition, although she saw nothing, even though the figure was chased by the family dog. Similarly, the maids refused to stay in one of the back rooms because of a presence that they could feel there. The rector carried out a ceremonial exorcism (of two ghosts rather than just one) on Christmas Day in 1937 and, although this solved the immediate problem, this seems to have been a temporary lull.

A later resident, Mrs Violet Tabor, a local JP, lived alone for many years after being widowed, when the building was no longer utilised as a rectory. Through the 1940s,'50s and early '60s, she had many sightings. Due to the fact that this lady was a magistrate, a council representative, school governor and Girl Guide Commissioner, her experiences should surely be taken seriously. Bear in mind that this was not a gloomy house, this was a house full of flowers, Persian rugs, and home baking in the country kitchen, so Violet Tabor's glimpses of the rectory ghost could not have been anticipated. The unidentified noises she heard at night were also not known to worry her unduly.

After a few years of living in what had been the gardener's cottage in the grounds, Mrs Tabor finally moved away from the area, and the rectory, which was by now in disrepair, was demolished. The 1962 workmen saw and heard a mysterious, shapeless figure moving around the passages and staircases, and opening and shutting doors. The men also found that timber and stones had been moved in their absence. The cellar was thought to be the destination for this shadowy figure, which was seen in daylight hours by several of the workers who had sat down in a dark corner to eat their lunches.

The demolition contractor at the time, Frederick Pope, was one of several witnesses, and his dog was reported to have been barking uncontrollably whenever it was brought onto the site. Pope even claimed that the same shadowy figure followed him home one evening. The rector from the 1930s compared notes with Mr Pope and their descriptions matched – his theory regarding Pope being followed was that the unknown ghost was unhappy about his home being demolished. This, presumably, could also be the explanation for a number of fires that were started during the demolition works, none of which could be explained in any other way.

In 1962, the rector of Sutton Church was asked to carry out another exorcism as he, too, had reported ghostly sights and sounds. However, he felt this was not really the work of a humble parish priest, and, rather astonishingly, Frederick Pope said he would take on the task himself. He claimed to have had experience when doing other work which involved renovating tombs. His methodology was interesting: a Bible reading in the ruins, after which he asked the troubled figure to follow him into the grounds, where he dug a shallow grave in the shelter of some trees. The ghost was not seen or heard again, and Frederick Pope claimed this was because he had found his final resting place.

Perhaps Mr Pope was right, because in July 1966 Warwick J. Rodwell wrote (in *Essex Countryside*) that he had taken part in

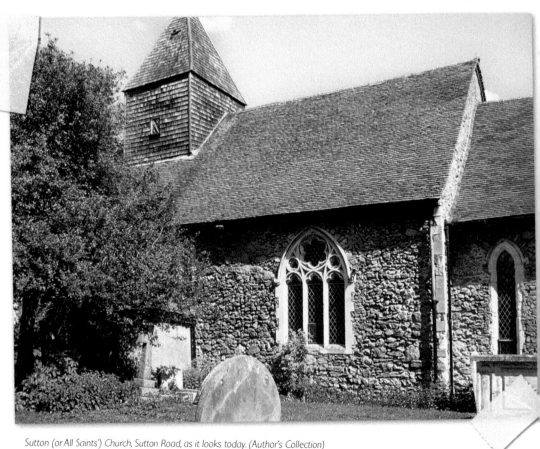

Sutton (or All Saints') Church, Sutton Road, as it looks today. (Author's Collection)

several organised ghost hunts in the vicinity, to no avail. David Hobbs of Ghost Hunters Extraordinaire was luckier – though some might not agree. He visited the nearby churchyard much more recently, and saw the apparition of a man hiding there, a man he described as frightened of Hell, because he (so the story goes) had killed his wife. However, this 'ghost' has also been exorcised, after the police were called in.

Readers interested in 'seeing' the church and churchyard should take a look at the youtube website where you can also hear, with a little imagination, what is described there as the 'grumpy graveyard ghost'. Although sometimes known as All Saints' Church, Sutton Church with its Norman origins should not be confused with the nineteenth-century All Saints' Church which is, even more confusingly, at the other end of Sutton Road in central Southend.

As for the site of the rectory, a Tudor-style manor house (Sutton Manor) was finally finished in the former grounds, with a galleried landing and oak panelling – and no ghosts.

Southchurch Rectory

This Grade II listed building in Southchurch Boulevard was inhabited from 1933 to 1941 by Canon Maurice Elphinstone. It was this man who was convinced that the rectory was haunted by someone who had held his post in an earlier decade – or even century. The former rector was described by the canon as being greedy and mercenary, and as such was doomed after death to roam the passages of the rectory at night. The apparition does not appear to have phased the canon, however, nor does it appear to have bothered subsequent incumbents.

St Clement's Church, Leigh-on-Sea

Known locally as Leigh Church, St Clement's Church dates back, in part, to the fifteenth century with an even earlier church on the site, so it is not surprising that it comes with a few ghost stories attached.

The main thrust of the sightings has been of small, flickering lights, thought to be the souls of the drowned, a theory endorsed by author Eric Maple, a member of the Folklore Society. The location of the church, off Leigh Hill, on a raised mound, offers striking views of the estuary, and, given its proximity to the Thames, and Leigh's fishing heritage, it is clear that incidents of drowning have not been uncommon in the history of the area. Memorials and graves of local fishermen are in plentiful supply in and around the church with local well-known names featuring prominently; the appropriately named families of Haddock and Salmon, and the Cotgroves.

In 1963, television producer John Kennedy Melling held a midnight vigil at the church for the BBC, but had no luck in pinning down any particular ghost or spectre of any kind. Perhaps another such vigil is now due.

St Nicholas' Church, Canewdon

There are more stories attached to this fourteenth-century (some sources say earlier) church, than any other in the local area. Canewdon village, recorded in the Domesday Book, lies some six miles to the north-east of Southend-on-Sea, and is surrounded by green belt. The church of St Nicholas lies at the western end of the village, set 128ft above the marshes, and

A recent photograph of St Clement's Church, Leigh. (Author's Collection)

its massive tower was a landmark for shipping. It is said that if someone circles the church alone at midnight, the witches and ghosts will come out and sing to them, or you could visit on Hallowe'en and, after running round the church three times anticlockwise, you could experience a spot of time travel. Certainly, the church – and village – attracts an inordinate amount of visitors on 31 October every year. The amount of people has often resulted in the police blocking off access to the church.

Members of the Phenomenist League, who organised a ghost hunt at the church in August 1957, were obviously disappointed that nothing like this happened when they tried the midnight walk themselves. They did, however, experience what was described as 'psychic cold' near the altar, and saw a weird 'aura of light' round the top of the church tower. More specifically, Eric Maple writes in *The Dark World of Witches* of an earlier period when an old woman from 'Dutch stock' was in the church lighting the lamps for evening service. She was disturbed by 'a misty figure [who] quietly entered and knelt in prayer before the altar'. This was another woman, 'faceless and wrapped in a grey shroud'. The old woman was not afraid, because she reasoned that if it was in the church, then perhaps it was an angel. She therefore knelt alongside the spectre to pray, but when she opened her eyes, the figure had vanished.

However, others have reported a number of more specific ghostly apparitions. There is the headless woman, dressed in silk, seen riding on a hurdle (a kind of sledge) down the hill from the church to the river where she disappears, but appears again

St Nicholas' Church, Canewdon, which dates back about 700 years. (Author's collection)

on the other side of the water. Then there is a woman with a poke bonnet (a witch?) who appears on moonless nights and travels through the west gate of the church, again towards the river, and appears to then walk across the water. It is said that anyone who approaches such a figure is lifted into the air and let down in the nearest ditch, but there are no reports of this actually happening (not that everything is reported). A young girl has also been seen waiting at the end of the vic-arage driveway, near to the entrance to the graveyard, and a 'grey lady' is said to wander

the graveyard. These could of course all be permutations of the same figure, described differently by different people, or it could be four separate apparitions.

Because this was witch territory during the time of the infamous seventeenth-century Essex witch trials, stories of ghosts are not unnaturally tied in with stories of witches. Legend has it that every time a stone falls from the tower of St Nicholas Church, one witch dies, to be replaced by another. There is also the legend – originating perhaps with Hadleigh (male) witch James 'Cunning' Murrell, the last witch doctor in England – that there will always be at least six witches in Canewdon, including three in silk and three in cotton (the latter equating to the less wealthy). One had to be the wife of the butcher, one of the baker, and one of the vicar!

The infamous male witch of Canewdon, George Pickingill (who died in the early twentieth century, fifty years after Murrell) was also known as the Master of Witches, the Wise Man of Canewdon and Master of the Canewdon Coven or even The Devil of Canewdon; obviously a figure to be reckoned with. Pickingill's contribution to the supernatural associations of the area was much darker, and he has been linked to several familiars, and to satanic rituals including nocturnal orgies in the churchyard with his Romany brethren! It seems that Canewdon witches' familiars were not the traditional black cats, but white mice, and a witch could not die until her mouse had found another owner who then inherited her powers.

When Chris Halton, an internationally-recognised medium and paranormal investigator visited St Nicholas in 2008, for Haunted Earth, he reported seeing a woman in white in the church, and a priest at the chancel end – a man in his forties with a white surplice and stern features, dating, he thought, from around the time of the First World War. He also got an image of an earlier male figure in a black frock coat with a white wig and walking stick. These sightings took place during broad daylight.

One of the investigators from mysterial. org.uk also visited the church during daylight hours, and felt gravel being thrown at him in the graveyard, although there was no one to be seen. In the graveyard, he had the sense that a woman was weaving in and out of the gravestones looking for something. Inside the church, he felt his throat being constricted, and his breathing affected, sensing something 'really bad' had happened. Following the incident he was told a story of a man hacking his wife and her lover to death in the very spot that he had breathing problems, but this story has been impossible to verify.

Even the renowned Derek Acorah and the *Most Haunted Live* television team turned up in April 2004 at St Nicholas to carry out a very public investigation. Will Storr in his *Will Storr vs the Supernatural* writes a sceptical account of this visit, when Derek made contact with a 'Matthew' but had trouble locating his surname, although everyone else around him was just waiting for him to say Hopkins (as in Witchfinder General), which he did, eventually. Yvette Fielding, the show's presenter, however, was very impressed.

A rather different ghost was identified by author Eric Maple when he visited Canewdon in the 1960s, accompanying members of The Ghost Club. He was interested in the ghost of a highwayman who was buried in the churchyard in 1795. The grave was described as the scene of a strange ritual, with village children dancing around it seven times to ensure it remained 'unquiet' because 'an unquiet ghost must always guard the other graves'; an interesting and inventive theory.

More factually, the church occupies a prominent, high, position, and could conceivably have served as a watch tower as well as a centre for worship during its long history. The most haunted locations of the church are its porch, its graveyard, and oddly, its car park. If only those bricks could talk …

(Note: for Hockley Church *see* section on Open Spaces, Hockley Woods.)

three

Haunted Commercial Buildings

Shops and offices have ghosts too, although they are not that commonplace. Such visitors from the past can of course turn up anywhere, and nowhere is immune.

Short Street/Queensway

B&Q was built on this site in 1987 (closed 2007) and a few years later, Wendy Pullman started working there as an early-morning cleaner. She recalls vividly one particular morning when she saw a coalman wearing a black-leather hat with an extended band behind his neck for extra protection – the sort of hat worn by coal-men of old. This was on the shop floor of the store, and other employees, although they did not see him, mentioned a feeling of overwhelming cold that came and went.

Wendy also saw a man walking through what appears to have been his original front door (at her time it was the bathroom area of B&Q), bearing in mind that this site had once housed a number of cottages that were demolished round about the 1970s. She recalls seeing other figures in the store and in what was the store's car park, all seeming to date from the same pre-war period.

An early coalman – and an unusual ghost.
(Image courtesy of Toby Williams)

As she is a practising clairvoyant, this is perhaps not too surprising, but what is interesting to note is that Kelly's Directory confirms the existence of a coal merchants in 1900 in this location – Moy Thomas Ltd – in addition to the Great Eastern Railway's own goodsyard, and this is a reference source of which Wendy was quite unaware.

High Street, Southend

Up to and including the 1970s, there was an ironmongers in the High Street, originally known as The Padlock, and later as Owen and Wallis (close to where Wallis' fashion store is now located). In around 1970, one of the sales assistants was Julie Rawlinson, and she had an experience there that she was still able to recall seventeen years later, in an article in the *Southend Echo*.

She was working in the toy department, above which was a stock room, often the source of unidentified footsteps. One day, when she was on the stairs leading to this room, in the process of putting stock away, she saw a man looking up at her with a large grin on his face. The door leading to the stairs was shut fast, and there had been no sound of his approach but what has stuck with Julie is that she couldn't see his legs. From the waist up, he seemed normal, with grey hair, perhaps in his fifties, but from the waist down … Julie looked again, but the figure had disappeared.

Concerned about what she had seen, Julie told the manager of her encounter – Mr Wallis – describing the man in as much detail as she could. To her surprise Mr Wallis became quite excited and pointed to three portraits hanging on an upstairs wall, asking her if she recognised anyone. Astonishingly, the answer was yes. One of the portraits was the very same man.

Mr Wallis told her that the man was his father, and the date was the anniversary of his death. The building had once been the Wallis family home, and the stock room had been the bedroom of Mr Wallis Senior, and the place that he had died. No wonder the experience remained for so long in Julie's memory.

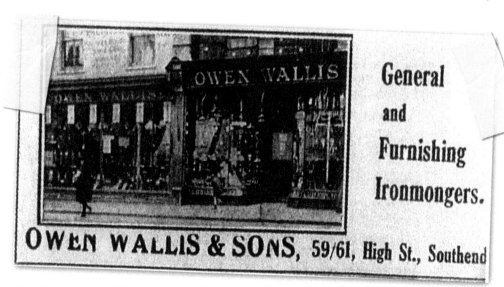

Owen Wallis advert, pre-1970. (Image courtesy of Southend Museums Service)

Nelson Street

This attractive and historic street is now the home of professional businesses such as solicitors and accountants. Between Nos 1-15 Nelson Street was the original focus of shopping in Southend prior to the development of the High Street. Built around 1860, it was then the shopping street for the 'new' Cliff Town Estate. But in the 1960s, No. 7 had housed Andrews E. Aynsley Ltd, manufacturers of Masonic regalia.

Most of the basements on this western side of the street were dark, dank places, the ideal location for unsavoury sights and sounds – but the cellar at No. 7 was in fact inhabited by a couple of men who made jewellery. These men reported to the staff upstairs that they had felt someone moving around, someone invisible to the naked eye, and Val Lawrence who was working upstairs recalled recently that everyone, including her, avoided going down those basement stairs. She, and the other staff, had similar experiences, and she still shudders at the memory all these years later. The current occupants have had no similar experiences, but admit that it is an area to be avoided!

Meteor Road

Over twenty-five years ago, Freda Gregory was working as a nurse in one of the nursing homes in the area – most of them are now rest homes or care homes, including those in Meteor Road. It was customary to sleep over when the shift required, and Freda was allocated a room at the top of

The west side of Nelson Street today. (Author's Collection)

the house in what would have been the Matron's quarters at one time.

She recalls on one occasion closing the window before settling down to sleep but had to get up again in the night because she could feel a cold draught. The window was now open. The mystery kept her awake for a while, but, when telling other nurses the next day, she discovered that she was not the only one who had had this experience.

Had someone – or something – come in, or gone out? And why choose the window? And why that window, the highest point of the house? A solid human form would surely choose an alternative option.

London Road (between Chalkwell Park and The Cricketers)

When author Wesley Downes gave a talk about ghosts and hauntings to the Westcliff Women's Institute in the 1960s, one of the members had a story for him that he had not come across before. He was able to add to the information by visiting another witness, both of these ladies having worked together in a café in London Road in the 1920s.

Above this café had been an art studio complete with resident artist, along with a school teaching music (courtesy of Leslie, a music arranger) and drama (courtesy of Elsie, an actress and producer). It was Elsie who first saw an unpleasant vision in the kitchen, in the presence of the other teachers, who saw nothing. She described what she'd seen as a pale, thin young man aged about twenty with untidy sandy hair and an unshaven face, who had appeared through the open door and ran out when she screamed.

When Elsie checked with the estate agents, she discovered that a young man, described in those days as an 'imbecile', had died a few months before the studio opened, prompting his parents to move away. The description seemed to fit.

Subsequently, the others began to see ghostly shapes, culminating in all three of them clearly seeing the figure Elsie had described. Their conclusion was that this spirit, or ghost, did not have the mental capacity to realise he was dead, and they used their own combined thought processes to 'project' their sympathy and their objections to his presence, which had worried Elsie in particular. This seems to have done the trick, and after some months of less frequent appearances, he was never seen again. The power of thought, or the power of multiple minds working together, or perhaps mind over spectral matter. Wesley reached no conclusions.

Broadway West

On the Paranormal Database there is a report of the bakery here being haunted. It refers to a man who committed suicide before the site was converted to a bakery, and this is the man who has been blamed, so to speak, for a number of later manifestations. There was talk of objects being moved, puzzling footsteps and unexplained breezes – but nothing in recent years. This is one ghost who has apparently disappeared, literally, of his or her own accord.

four

Haunted Open Spaces

While dark rooms and shadows can spawn visitations, the supernatural world is not restricted to interiors. Woods are a popular spot, as are country lanes, subways and busy highways – there's nowhere free from the past.

Queensway/Southchurch Road junction

At this busy junction in the heart of Southend is a contemporary, brick-built subway, giving access to Sutton Road in the

'Ratman' Underpass in the heart of Southend. (Image courtesy of Bradly Vaughn)

north, and the Mayor's House, Porters, in the east. It has, and does, provide shelter for the local homeless on occasion.

One such man was unlucky in that he was targeted here by a group of bullies and left without his blanket in the middle of winter, resulting in his death (presumably from hypothermia). This story has the additional grim detail that the man's face was gnawed by rats after his death … and it is this horrific coda that has given rise to the story of the ghost that haunts this subway, known as the Ratman.

Bradley Vaughn's friends from school-days would report back that they had heard screams during the night, and the sounds of long nails scraping on the wall. Other stories have evolved of a mutant rat being seen and/or a hunched, snarling figure with yellow teeth. More recently, in July 2010, there was an entry on the *Echo News Forum* detailing the sound of scratching in this tunnel, like fingernails scraping on stone.

True? False? A ghost? A rat? Either way, a place to avoid after dark!

Junction Southend Arterial Road/Prince Avenue (Kent Elms Corner)

This ghost is particularly well known locally. It is said to be the ghost of a young girl killed in a car accident. 'She' appears bare-foot and muddy at the junction, hitching a ride to Victoria Circus in the town centre. A number of motor-cyclists have claimed to have seen her, stopped for her, and given her a lift – to find an empty seat behind them when they reached their destination. The missing girl must come as an almighty shock for any Good Samaritan involved, and perhaps an even bigger shock to then find that the pillion rider was a ghost.

Eastern Esplanade

Clairvoyant Wendy Pullman has had some interesting sightings in the area near the old gasworks (near Sea Life Centre). There are still remains of an old wooden jetty here, and Wendy has 'seen' men working on it wearing high-waisted trousers and caps; all similarly dressed in some kind of 'uniform'. These men did not appear to have been fishermen, which would have been predictable, because she saw them loading their boats with boxes. Who were they? When? What were they doing? Many possible answers spring to mind, but Wendy has no answers – she saw what she saw, and more than once, but does not attempt to explain it.

It is near to this very same spot that a report is recorded of a driver crashing his vehicle after swerving to avoid someone who had suddenly appeared in front of him in the road. To his relief, there was no body, no victim, when he extricated himself from

Mysterious orb under Southend jetty. (Image courtesy of Dave Bullock at Community Archive)

his vehicle – so what had he seen? Was one of the workers from the past life of the old jetty crossing the road?

More recently, when Dave Bullock from Prittlewell was taking photos of the jetty area a few years ago, he captured what could be described as a 'ghostly orb' in one of his images. Again, there are alternative possible explanations out there, but that makes (at least) three independent witnesses; too many to be a coincidence?

Leigh Road

The pond that was once a feature here (near the junction with The Broadway) has now been built on, but not without a struggle. Known as the Doom (or Witches') Pond, it was traditionally regarded as a ducking pond for witches. This was where witches were alleged to have been dragged by rope to see if they drowned, proving their innocence, or survived, proving they were witches, followed by the appropriate punishment, usually hanging.

If there is any truth in this, then of the three women tried as witches in Leigh-on-Sea, Joan Rowle is the most likely to have suffered this fate because she was tried in 1645 during the reign of Matthew Hopkins, the Witchfinder General who favoured this particular test. Although there are claims that Leigh's very own witch, Sarah Moore,

was dunked here, she did not die until the middle of the nineteenth century, long after such practices had died out.

With this kind of reputation, it is not surprising that black 'shapes' and shadows have been seen here, and it was at one time a place to be avoided after dark – before the days of street lighting, this part of Leigh Road was known locally as the 'darkest lane in Essex'. Even the murky waters of the 'pond' were said to be cursed, but what happened to any unfortunate animal that took a drink is not recorded.

A number of attempts at building on this site failed, due to its damp foundations

Site of the Witches' (or Doom) Pond in Leigh-on-Sea. (Image courtesy of Wes Downes and Ian Yearsley)

Untitled mosaic seemingly marking the site at Doom Pond.
(Author's collection)

and its instability — or, some would say, due to the curse. The pond was even reputed at one time to be bottomless, and also had a more prosaic claim to fame when it was used for washing products from the Leigh Pottery, once close by. However, persistence paid off in the end with a block of apartments now established, and there is no longer any sign of the pond, the ghosts, or the witches. There is, however, an attractive unlabelled mosaic in the vicinity, which seems to mark the 'spot' but without explanation.

Rochford Lake

A team of paranormal investigators, Spirit Finders, posted information on line and on youtube a few years ago regarding their visit to this location. The team included more than one medium, and they picked up a number of spirit entities around the edges of the lake.

The name Eleanor, apparently a victim of a witch hunt, was identified, being pulled along as if in a procession, tied with thick rope, and subsequently hanged after being dunked in the lake. Even more unpleasantly, there was the presence of an old woman who enjoyed watching others suffer, and who seemed to be suggesting that others were being punished when she was the one practising witchcraft.

Other spirits were of a man tied to a tree, and of a young boy who drowned accidentally in the lake. The group spent the night there, oblivious to the night fishing taking place in the vicinity, although the area with the most activity was not, interestingly, the area chosen by the fishermen. They collected some fascinating images on film, but it was not within their brief to investigate further, i.e. to track down local witches. While records of witch trials include Rochford witches, they do not include anyone called Eleanor, although there is a seventeenth-century 'widow' Hingson of Rochford identified, minus a Christian name.

The area, along with much of Essex, was at the centre of the seventeenth- and eighteenth-century witch trials, following Henry VIII's statute against witchcraft. It was a busy farming area just north of Southend when the latter was still a tiny hamlet at the south end of Prittlewell (the Witchfinder General, Matthew Hopkins, an Essex man, found many of his victims just a few miles away, in Canewdon).

Hockley Woods and Church Road, Hockley

When Wendy Pullman was out walking her dogs early in the morning – at around 7 a.m. before the local horse riders use the area – she heard the sound of horses' hooves. There was nothing to be seen, no extra-early riders, but the sound of the hooves was clear. She used the path from the car park to an open square, a favourite spot for dog walkers. It has not deterred her, or her dogs, from returning to the woods, however, which is certainly a beautiful and peaceful spot so close to the hubbub of Southend, and has echoed to the sound of horses and riders for centuries.

Nevertheless, there are other areas of the woods that Wendy avoids because she feels very uncomfortable, bearing in mind her clairvoyant status. Some of these are strictly no go because even the dogs don't want to venture there.

Contributors to the Ghost Hunters Extraordinaire website also make a number of references to sightings in Hockley Woods. One particular story which crops up regularly is of the disembodied voice of a 'shrieking boy' said to have had an unpleasant death – but this particular sound seems to have been proved to be that of a rather vocal owl.

There are a number of written accounts of a stage-coach (possibly from the early nineteenth century) crashing into a tree in nearby Church Road, Hockley, resulting in the death of the coachman and his lady passenger. The aftermath of this event is the frequent sighting of a phantom coach with four white horses passing near Hockley Church. The coach is said to stop, and the lady inside then waves her hand before the coach moves on, the horses swerve, and the crash is re-enacted.

In August, 1956, the local branch of the Phenomenist Research League (who met regularly in Fairfax Drive, Westcliff) set up a vigil in the graveyard of Hockley Church, and reported it as the most eerie place they had ever visited. They described the atmosphere as 'unearthly' and recounted hearing 'peculiar' sounds. More than one of the group saw a 'large white unidentified figure' but whether this is linked to the unlucky lady in the coach is not at all clear.

Hockley Church. A vigil was held in the graveyard in 1956. (Author's collection)

Continuing a little further north, St Andrew's Church tops this steep hill overlooking Canewdon a mile and a half away; also known as Ashingdon Minster. This is the church said to have been built on the orders of Canute, following his victory over Edmund Ironside at the Battle of Ashingdon in October 1016, 'for the souls of the men who there were slain' and the cemetery area is reputed to be the site of this famous battle. Its location is now sometimes called Haunted Hill.

There are several quite different hauntings ascribed to the area around the hill. One is of the ghosts of dying soldiers, especially around the anniversary (18 October) of the battle. As this was one of the bloodiest battles between the Anglo-Saxons and the Danes, this is not surprising. Legend has it that no grass grows where so much blood was spilt, but in fact someone has managed to bypass this, and the hill sports a plentiful array of green grass.

However, August does seem to be the most likely month to see this particular phenomenon, although it has also been spotted on Christmas Eve.

St Andrew's Church, Ashingdon, on 'Haunted Hill'. (Author's collection)

Although several people have, additionally, told of hearing screams in the lane that winds past the church, these screams are attributed to two different causes. One is a claim that a woman hanged herself from a tree since cut down, and it is her cries that can be heard. Another is of two men having a heated argument while walking along this lane, resulting in the death of one; his killer is said to have ended up in an asylum where he committed suicide, and it is his – not the victim's – cries that can be heard. The choice is yours.

Baker's Corner, Wakering

Also known as Baker's Grave, this is reputedly where a baker from Barling hanged himself from a prominent tree, a tree which has since been uprooted and replaced with housing. According to Jessie Payne, who has written much about Essex, there was a Clement le Bakere who lived in Wakering in 1314, so this may have been the man.

Until the mid-nineteenth century, suicides were not buried in consecrated ground, so the man was buried at the crossroads. It was then common practice for such bodies to be buried with a stake through their hearts to prevent their spirits escaping, but if this was the case, it patently did not work, because the spirit of 'Mr' Baker is said to still haunt the crossroads.

More specifically, on windy nights, the sound of his heels knocking together as he swung on the branch was said to be clearly audible – at least until the tree (between Barrow Hall Road and Little Wakering Road) was removed. It was also said that if you ran a hundred times around this tree, you would see the baker kneading his dough, but no one is known to have completed a hundred circuits.

Paglesham Road, Paglesham

Over the northern border of Southend, Paglesham, on the other side of the River Roach, was a hot-spot locally for smugglers. One particular hiding place, for such goodies as silk, was in the hollowed elm trees that stood in Paglesham Road near the bend that leads to East Hall (shown with its moated enclosure in Chapman and Andre's map of 1777).

Since the 'trade' disappeared, thanks to draconian legislation and the increased numbers of customs officers and coastguard stations, these trees have taken on a new role – as the site of hauntings, although the spectres are unidentified. Smugglers do seem to be the most likely candidates, given the reputation of Paglesham, and of those trees in particular, which could house as much as £200 worth of fabric. Not all the trees are left *in situ*, and the same could be said of the ghosts.

It is interesting that there are not more ghostly smugglers from the past who re-visit current-day Paglesham, but then not all such events are in the public domain.

The Smugglers Elms. (Image courtesy of Mark Roberts, from the Wiseman archive)

North of Southend, south of Hockley, this is a lesser-known region which featured in the Domesday Book. Two ghosts have featured here, although in recent rather than ancient times.

In the 1960s, Eric Maple wrote in *Essex Countryside* of a ghost seen swinging backwards and forwards in the wind, on the site of what seems to have been one of many early gibbets. Early in the current century, there was also more than one report of a 'glowing' entity that floated through the camping area off Holyoak Lane (used by scouting troupes from all over the country). These sightings were brief, without explanation, but veer more towards ghostly apparitions than, say, UFOs.

Hanging man – a sight leaving a lasting impression.
(Image courtesy of www.clipart.com)

There is a tale linked to this bleak area at the mouth of the Thames, told by Ian Yearsley in issue no. 5 of *Ghosts and Hauntings*. It involves two boys sleeping in the loft of an empty house. It seems they heard an argument taking place between a man and a woman, and then what sounded like the sort of screams associated with murder. The boys did not intervene, however, but kept their heads down, and when they finally emerged, when everything was quiet – there was nothing to be seen. Not only was there no body, no blood, but there was not even a sign of a struggle.

A murder from the past? Or not one but two vivid imaginations? Take your pick.

Barling

A few miles north of Little Wakering and south of Paglesham lies the even smaller village of Barling. It seems that at the beginning of the twentieth century a widow lived here who took her dog for a walk around the village every evening at the same time. On returning to her house after such a walk one night, she was attacked by burglars, resulting in her abrupt and unexpected death, and sightings of this old lady around the village have been sporadic over the years.

One particular sighting is recorded on the mysterial.org.uk website. In November of 1987 or 1988, a driver actually thought he had hit an 'old lady in period clothing, and a dog' who had appeared in his headlights directly in front of his car. The figures had appeared solid but there had been no bump, and when he left his car to check out the surroundings, there was nothing to be seen. This had an ongoing effect on the

Foulness Island – bleak and lonely, it hides its secrets well. (Author's Collection)

driver, who was still writing about it seventeen years later. Although he returned to the scene on several occasions, he has not witnessed a repeated sighting, but this does not affect his conviction about what he saw.

Foulness Island

Only accessible (by road) from Shoeburyness or Wakering, this mysterious island of less than a hundred houses, owned by the MOD, is full of secrets. Not just military secrets, although this is a place for testing weaponry which is reached via a security checkpoint.

In the 1990s, the editor of the now defunct *Ghosts and Hauntings* wrote of a local man some twenty years earlier who was giving his daughter a driving lesson on the island. Both saw a figure standing beside the road, dressed in what seemed to be a wartime demob suit, with a gabardine mackintosh and a trilby hat. Because of his unusual attire, they decided to have a closer look. But after turning the car around and retracing their journey, there was no sign of the man, and, more importantly, there was nowhere that he could possibly have gone. No hills or houses to hide behind, no woods or mist to disappear into, just a wide empty space.

There is also an empty farmhouse, which has a long-lost tale of domestic tragedy in its history. All that remains is an eerie atmosphere, apparent to every visitor, susceptible or otherwise. Is the headless woman seen at a lonely street corner in the vicinity connected to this 'tragedy' – or did two and two make five?

Foulness Sands in busier days. (Peter Owen collection)

Canewdon

Apart from its church and its pub, other parts of this small, atmospheric village have ghost stories to offer, at least one of which may be linked to the area's witches. Gardeners Lane has been the scene of a 'small patch of black mist' which has worried more than one driver. Could it be a witch, or even a witch's ghost?

Not far away, and offering a more solid phenomenon, there have been several sightings of a Crusader (late 1960s, 1970s) in the Larkhill Road area. Certainly battles were fought close by in the time of the Romans and in the time of Canute, and the figure may have been mistakenly identified … Identifying a ghost is never easy, let's face it.

Canewdon Pond in Lambourne Hall Road is another area where the ghost that has been seen drifting towards the crossroads has been identified as a witch. Richard Felix speculates on his *Ghosts of Essex* DVD that this could be one of the witches drowned by Matthew Hopkins during his reign of terror. The thinking behind his theory certainly makes sense. John Saunders, writing in *Essex Countryside* in October 2000, had a different theory; he felt that this was a witch who had been hanged, and denied burial in the churchyard.

Yet another theory, posited by Wesley Downes in issue no. 5 of *Ghosts and Hauntings*, is that a witch was buried at a crossroads in the village with a stake driven through her heart. The stake then fell out or worked loose (or may have missed its target in the first place) allowing the witch's spirit to wander freely and to return to the place she had known in life.

This particular article also refers to another quite different ghostly figure, although its location is in much the same vicinity. Not a witch, but a rather eccentric old lady riding a bicycle with one handlebar, just as she had been known to do in life.

A small village with a lot of stories.

A hundred years ago Canewdon – a village full of stories.
(Author's collection)

Wallasea Island

The marshes here are supposedly haunted by legendary witch 'Old Mother Redcap' and also by a maid who committed suicide by drowning. The poor girl had fallen pregnant by the master of the local manor house, who had thrown the poor girl out. 'Which house?' remains an unanswered question. (In the eighteenth century, for instance, less than a half dozen houses were recorded but this does not make the question any easier to answer.)

Even the generally strait-laced historian Philip Benton wrote of an area known at one time as 'Lucky Corner' which was not so lucky for the 'woman without a head' whose apparition was seen there 300 years ago. This could easily be the same figure that appeared at Foulness.

Others have seen a phantom ship crossing a part of the island which is now land, but was once water. The waters around here have many stories to tell of wrecked ships, but again 'Which ship?' remains unanswered.

A phantom ship – offering an alternative kind of ghost.
(Image courtesy of www.clipart.com)

five

Haunted Watering Holes

This chapter is devoted to local pubs, hotels, and a restaurant. There are others that want to keep their ghosts under wraps to avoid deterring customers. Although some could of course be attracted! Which ones? That would be telling.

Bakers Bar, Alexandra Street

This building is now a nightclub with a different name, but was built in 1850 as a bakery. It continued as a working bakery until around 1926 and has since had a variety of face lifts over the years (a bikers' café in the 1960s for instance). However, a few years after Bakers Bar opened in 1990, the BBC's Shaun Peel interviewed Victor Room, an employee, following Bakers Bar's nomination as the BBC Essex Pub of the Week. This recording is available on audio cassette at the Essex Record Office at Chelmsford, and has some fascinating, and relevant, material, reproduced with the BBC's permission.

The bar was, at that time, a jazz bar, and Victor described a small door (opposite the old ABC cinema) which gave access to a vast underground open space. It would often be as late as 2.30 a.m. when Victor left the building after locking up, and this was the time when he would regularly hear the sound of a time clock 'pinging'. There was an old clock in the basement which had to be the source of the sound. However, it seems that this clock had not been used since the premises were utilised as a bakery

Image of a baker in the early morning.
(Image courtesy of www.clipart.com)

when the employees would clock in and out, and which, as far as Victor was aware, no longer worked.

Victor's theory was that this was the sound of one such employee clocking in, as the time would have been appropriate for someone making bread early in the morning ready for the shop to open. He could visualise someone getting his overalls on and getting his flour out, ready for the working day, but this was more what he sensed than a sighting of an actual image.

The only back-ups for this particular story are interesting to note – a nursery that was at one time offered the basement as accommodation but declined on the grounds that it felt 'spooky'; and the site has also been visited by a medium who felt the presence of two different spirits, a visit recounted by the current club's Operations Manager (at time of writing).

Boston Hall Hotel, The Leas

This building overlooking the sea is no longer a hotel, but it has an interesting past. In 1973, for instance, a young couple booked a room after a cut-price evening of amusement arcades, chips and coca-cola (the discarded coke can plays a role in their story).

In the early hours, they woke up at the same time, not sure what had woken them, but feeling cold, and then aware of the sound of 'old-fashioned' music, perhaps 'from a spinet' (harpsichord) or similar instrument – but coming from inside the room. Next was the sound of footsteps in the room, followed by a very loud sound of metal on metal – the sound of a coca-cola can being thrown into the bin. The couple decided they had had enough, put on the lights, dressed, and left.

The original Boston Hall Hotel, looking completely harmless. (Paddy Ballard Collection)

Some years later, the hotel was burnt out, left derelict and was boarded up. As a result, it attracted its quota of young lads who would break in to the empty premises to play games of tag. One boy made his way to an upstairs floor which had only a few joists remaining – risking life and limb to peer out of the window at his pals outside – only to feel someone tap him on the shoulder. He looked around but there was no one there. Then a male voice clearly said, 'It's burning'. Not surprisingly, the boy didn't stay to hear any more.

While it is difficult to be completely sure that these two stories refer to the same hotel, the contributors to the *Mystery Mag* website were certainly convinced that this had to be more than just a coincidence.

The Cricketers, London Road

In the local *Standard Recorder* of the 4 January 1973, there was a grim account of a suicide. Leslie Middleton drenched himself in petrol and set fire not only to himself but to two crowded bars. The newspaper used the words 'went up like a bomb' to describe the incident, which was attended by twenty fire fighters, although luckily no one else was injured. Apparently, according to the then landlord, Mr Middleton had threatened this action on more than one occasion, but no one had taken him seriously.

It seems that this event triggered a number of strange incidents in the pub, which were thought to be caused by a poltergeist. The staff now found furniture upturned, bottles and boxes in the wrong place, and similar unexplained happenings – not just once but on a regular basis. Whether this had anything to do with Mr Middleton is a matter of conjecture. What is known is

that the mysterious activities stopped once the pub was dramatically renovated.

Royal Hotel, High Street

The Royal is a historic building dating from the eighteenth century, and set prominently on the corner of Southend High Street and Royal Terrace. There have been a couple of paranormal investigations here, but the management at time of writing do not have access to the results.

However, Tonio Perrot, who lives locally, remembers seeing an image of a small group of men in tricorn hats reflected in one of the hotel's mirrors on a visit there some years ago. A look round the room

Tricorned individual enjoying his high-status lifestyle. (Image courtesy of www.clipart.com)

confirmed that there was no one fitting that description anywhere near. These hats were of course eighteenth-century headwear for high-status individuals, and Lord Nelson, who visited Lady Hamilton at Southend at the beginning of the nineteenth century, is famously portrayed wearing such a hat.

As a fashionable assembly room during the early nineteenth century, with royal visitors including Princess Caroline, this reflected image does seem to have been very much a brief glimpse of the past, rather than a substantiated image of what was the present. Whether the great naval hero himself visited the Royal is open to conjecture.

It also seems that the basement here, now full of music and life, was once a dark and spooky place which all but the bravest would avoid. This, however, is probably true of dark basements everywhere.

Oscar's, Leigh Hill

This three-storey building (no longer Oscar's, the 1990s restaurant) was built at the beginning of the twentieth century. The story goes that one of its earliest inhabitants was a young woman who was deserted by her sailor lover. After years of waiting for him, she is said to have locked herself up in a room on the top floor and lived as a recluse. This story convinced the restaurant's manager (in 1990), Alan Hugo, that he had found an explanation for the ghost that was scaring him and his staff, and the owner, Colin Boxer, was similarly persuaded.

Mr Hugo had taken to calling the ghost Amy, and felt she was responsible for mirrors being pulled down, bedclothes being slashed, and even claw-marks on men's backs. He felt that Amy was taking some

kind of revenge for those lost years, but he was angered by her unwanted presence and by the damage that she was incurring. The bedroom which was used by Mr Boxer was said to have been originally 'Amy's' and this was where there was a noticeable chill – the previous owners had even woken one morning to find their bedspread slashed. As a result, Mr Boxer kept an Alsatian dog which slept in the room at night – but the dog had taken to waking up howling in the night for no apparent reason.

The barman had actually seen a woman who could have been Amy – at a party when someone flitted past him. Because he didn't recognise her, he did a double take, but she was then nowhere to be seen. As for Mr Hugo, he complained of hearing loud and frequent unexplained crashes, and of the lights going out time after time, although there seemed to be no problem with the fuses. His theory was that Amy was

The reclusive ghost at Oscar's window, waiting ... and waiting ... (Image courtesy of Toby Williams)

a bitter visitation who hated men because her lover had abandoned her.

Mr Boxer was naturally worried about the effect such stories could have on his customers, and called in Carla Richards, described by the *Standard Recorder* (11 May 1990) as a 'chain-smoking psychic'. Carla, it seems, was not convinced about the torn bedspread, feeling uncut toe-nails was a more likely explanation! She also pooh-poohed a photograph of 'the ghost' that the *Recorder* had printed, preferring to get her own insights via her invisible spirit companion (Norman) and from handling a brick used in the original building.

The brick released a series of moving images that only Carla could see – she had already felt the presence of a suicide, and the images now showed her a girl hurling herself from the upstairs window into the back-yard. This yard remained a sinister and gloomy place, forming a damp sunless shaft, almost a pit, at the back of the building. Carla felt the timing was probably the 1920s/1930s and that this was someone whose mother had kept her 'almost a prisoner' until she had been run over and killed by a tram, at which point the daughter had ended her own life. Carla felt that both women, not just the daughter, were haunting the place, the daughter effectively 'forcing' her mother to stay on, and the two of them at loggerheads in death as they were in life.

The psychic carried out an exorcism soon afterwards, and this was pretty much the end of the story. Except that an unidentified female from an earlier age is still seen from time to time looking out of a top-floor window.

Shoeburyness Hotel

A film crew from Anglia Television visited this listed Victorian structure in 2003 for a programme on Britain's most haunted buildings. The then manageress reeled off all manner of sightings in an interview with an *Evening Echo* reporter – a lady in a wheel-chair, a man in the cellar, a man snoring, and a little girl and boy in Victorian outfits.

The Victorian girl was seen not just by manageress, Alison Bart, but by two of her children. Alison also told of an occasion when the ghost did one of her chores; she had left a huge pile of laundry out ready for the next day, and when she came down-stairs to tackle it, it had been washed and folded up!

Cindy, one of the barmaids, had also got used to hearing footsteps on the stairs when she was in the cellar – initially this was a frightening experience, but she, along with the rest of the staff, got used to their unseen visitor after a while. Another bar-maid, Lisa, saw the image of a man in the cellar (and had a witness to his presence) who promptly disappeared, and had heard unidentified sounds when staying in one of the bedrooms. Lisa also found that the kitchen was in a mess upon her arrival on one occasion although she had tidied eve-rything away the night before, so perhaps there was indeed more than one ghost – one house-proud, and one the reverse.

Unusually, these bizarre happenings were accepted by everyone as a natural occur-rence, and neither customers nor staff seemed daunted by the odd goings on. The hotel has been closed and boarded up since a fire in 2004 but is set for redevelopment as housing. No doubt in its new guise this site will have been exorcised of its past.

Shoeburyness Hotel, with a stagecoach outside and a family of ghosts inside. (Image courtesy of www.footstepsphotos.co.uk)

The Sarah Moore, Elm Road, Leigh

This pub was named after the last witch alleged to be ducked in Doom Pond, about half a mile east (*see* Open Spaces section). Sarah Moore, who died in 1867, was known locally as the Sea Witch, and it didn't do to antagonise her. She was blamed for cursing unborn children with a harelip if the mother had upset her, with causing storms at sea in revenge against skippers who crossed her, and with spontaneously combusting children who had tried to break in to her home on Victoria Wharf.

Sarah had a useful source of income. As sailors boarded their ships, she extended a claw-like hand and screamed out 'Buy a fair wind, buy a fair wind. ' Sailors, during this period, were said to be superstitious and few argued with her, regarding a few pence as a form of cheap insurance. Glyn Morgan gives a particularly fascinating account in his

book, *Essex Witches*, of a captain, unknown to the area, who refused to pay, and even laughed at the old crone. When torrential rain, thunder and lightning alarmed every

An earlier pub sign depicting Sarah Moore.
(Image courtesy of Mark Kimber)

one of his experienced deckhands after they had put to sea, even the skipper listened to their cries of 'witches' work'. He rushed to the bows and shouted 'I'll kill the witch,' and struck the prow three times. Sarah is reputed to have died shortly afterwards, with three bloody gashes in her head. This is just the sort of bloody death that would precede ghostly visitations.

The pub originally had a sign depicting Sarah (without her hook nose) as a kind of early bag lady, and she is regarded as the ghost who is said to haunt Bell Wharf in Leigh's Old Town. Interestingly in 2000, when this pub sign was removed, and replaced by a bland name-only sign following its refurbishment some very odd things began to happen. The acting manager, Jenny Smith, started to hear strange noises – of footsteps, mainly – and witnessed glasses 'falling' off shelves, seemingly of their own accord. She also had problems with new equipment breaking down, and even with an unexpected internal flooding.

Was the foul-mouthed Sarah unhappy about the removal of her image? Or had the renovations disturbed someone else, someone not connected with the witch? Answers on a postcard please!

Marlborough Head Inn, West Street, Rochford

Here on the northern border of Southend in 2006, Ghost Hunters Extraordinaire were asked by the landlord to carry out an investigation. This old inn had been experiencing some strange happenings: heavy footsteps, cold spots in the bar area, and noises from an empty room on the first floor. The team arrived at 10 p.m. and spent three hours on site, concentrating on the downstairs rooms as per their brief.

While three of the team (including a clairvoyant) settled down for a cup of coffee, others set up an electro-magnetic field reader by the main bay window. It wasn't long before at least two of the coffee-drinkers felt a physical presence actually touching them – seemingly to attract their attention. The clairvoyant could see one of her colleagues in a 'waterlogged dark cloak', and could additionally sense the presence of an 'important' man connected to a ship or ships, an agitated figure, with the date 1796 featuring.

The clairvoyant then felt a presence by the front door, which she investigated, coming back to report a name – Steven Piper (interestingly, this is the same surname of the landlady recorded in 1848), and a date, 1539. This pre-dates the Marlborough Head, but it is very likely that an earlier pub was on the same site. She also visited the cellar, accompanied by two of her team, and was able to describe two children dressed in eighteenth-century clothing; another woman with a bonnet and white dress, perhaps a servant, was also spotted in the same location.

The group held a meditation shortly before midnight in the bar area, and the clairvoyant immediately felt a dark presence kneeling in front of her with a bloodied knife. Not surprisingly, this left her somewhat agitated. This was not the only presence – another of those involved could feel the presence of a man in a brown suit who was dying from a bee sting, and gave the name George Starkey. It seems that the clairvoyant knew of this man and of his rather unusual death.

Ghost Hunters Extraordinaire ended their investigation at the Marlborough Head shortly after midnight, and have not been called back since. They continue to investigate other worrying, or inexplicable, occurrences in the area, however, preserving privacy when required.

The Anne Boleyn, Southend Road, Rochford

Although this public house was not built until 1901, there have been tales of sightings of Anne Boleyn, whose family had a home close by. She would have ridden in the local woods along with King Henry and his entourage. Anne Boleyn, in fact, is reputed to haunt so many places in Essex, Kent and Norfolk – not to mention the Tower of London – that she must be the busiest ghost in England.

However, a very different sighting, which took place just yards from the pub, early on a Thursday morning in recent years, was when Wendy Pullman (a clairvoyant) saw a little girl of some four or five years old walking along the pavement. She was wearing patent black shoes, with curly brown hair past her shoulders, and was neat and tidy in a dated (Victorian or Edwardian) fashion. The girl disappeared after just a few minutes, and Wendy's husband had to admit that he had seen nothing – i.e. the girl was not living flesh and blood.

It is interesting to speculate as to whether this was the same young child said to have been seen, briefly, sitting in one of the windows of the pub in 2001 (by the then owner Dave Smith and his wife, Angela). According to an interview they gave in the *Evening Echo* of the 9 August that year, their grandson didn't like sleeping on the premises because of 'something'. Not only that, but on more than one occasion, after locking up the function room, it was unlocked upon their return the next morning.

Anne Boleyn pub sign, an iconic representation. (Image courtesy of Mark Kimber)

The White Hart, High Street, Great Wakering

When Gavin Lyon's father was landlord here (prior to 1996), Gavin – and other members of staff – reported seeing a hooded man. The story goes that there was a murder here in around 1840, when a man was killed with a fire-iron which was kept near a large open fire. As this timbered building is over 400 years old, it is not surprising that at least one ghost story is attached to it.

The Anchor, High Street, Canewdon

When Richard Felix, self-styled Ghost Hunter General, visited The Anchor when making his *Ghosts of Essex* DVD in 2006, he was able to talk to one of the regulars who had actually felt something – cold and undefinable, but certainly 'something' – when working through the night in the pub, painting the ceiling.

Other stories he heard – of a young girl in Puritan costume – were hearsay, but have been reported on more than one occasion by different people, people who had probably not heard the story before. She had been seen in the dining area of the pub, and in one of the upstairs rooms, and had been christened Sara.

This follows an investigation six years earlier reported in the *Evening Echo* which offered an alternative name for the girl, after being visited by a medium/psychic from Ankhara Psychic Services. Then named as Catherine, it seems that she had been imprisoned by a wicked uncle in 1660 during the time of the Witchfinder General, Matthew Hopkins. The frightened girl had died after being treated in the local village as a witch but there is no further information as to how she met her end.

The Anchor has been the subject of other investigations, including one by Paranormal Dimensions for the BBC programme, *Inside Out*, in 2004. This reported that staff had seen flying remote controls, heard mysterious baby cries and detected the aroma of unexplained perfume – even knives had been said to travel across the kitchen. The team here came up with an optional version of the 'Sara' story – that she had an affair with a wealthy landowner at an earlier period (sixteenth century) and became pregnant, with the result that she was locked away in the building that became The Anchor. Methods of investiga-

Anchor Inn, Canewdon, home to the mysterious 'lady in red'. (Image courtesy of Ron Bowers)

tion here, as with other similar teams, were very high-tech. They used electro-magnetic field detectors and infrared cameras that can record Orbs, the latter being areas of 'light' believed to be the spirits of the dead. With the help of such technology, and the input of a local medium, their findings seem not only scientific, but objective. 'Hard evidence' as such was, however, difficult to come by.

As recently as February 2010, Ron Bowers, the psychic photographer, visited The Anchor, and produced some fascinating pictures, with a small group of people present. He had no pre-knowledge of the history of the pub, which is the way he prefers to work, so the photograph – which features what he describes as a lady wearing red clothing – is particularly impressive.

The pub becomes particularly crowded at Hallowe'en when it is invaded by ghost-hunters (and non-believing revellers) from miles around. When writer and traveller Bernie Friend visited The Anchor on 31 October 2008, he managed to speak to the landlord, John Amey, and wrote about his visit in the *Southend Echo*. Mr Amey revealed that the pub was a courthouse over 400 years ago where condemned witches would be tried before being sent to the ducking pond and stocks outside the church. He had no personal paranormal experiences – although it seems his wife did – but this is probably irrelevant. No doubt the stories, and the investigations, formal and informal, will continue unabated for the foreseeable future.

Rayleigh Lodge, The Chase

This has been a pub since the mid-twentieth century – currently offering Thai food – but was formerly a private house, apparently starting life as the gate house of a mansion built for Henry VIII – perhaps to entertain Anne Boleyn. Queen Elizabeth I also stayed at the Lodge, which was convenient for local hunting; hence its Grade II listed status.

Staff here often referred to the ghost of a young woman in long dress and hat – as well as more vague stories of a 'scary' cellar. Customers, too, reported seeing someone disappearing between two bars, plus a mystifying 'pink mist' in the garden – such experiences perhaps linked to this same, seemingly historic (but not Anne Boleyn this time) phantom figure. One manager, Bryan Matthews, who had instigated structural work in the pub, felt 'someone' brush past him up the stairs after the bar was closed for the night, and his wife felt cold fingers touch her shoulder. The family dog would only sleep outside his master's bedroom, but several exorcisms did not work.

The story behind the sightings goes back to an earlier century when a local girl drowned herself in a nearby pond after becoming pregnant by the Lord of the Manor. The fate of such girls, it seems, was relatively common place, but never happy.

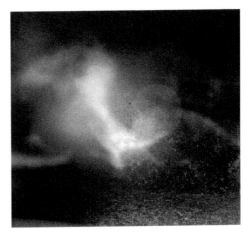

Misty, ethereal figure captured on film in Rayleigh. (Image courtesy of Leigh Lacey-Marques, www.s-o-sparanormal.co.uk)

The Garrison Arms, Campfield Road, Shoeburyness

The manager of what was formerly the 'Captain Mannering', in the 1990s, 'often heard children playing and laughing in the afternoons when the pub was shut'. Originally, he thought this came from the playground of the adjacent school, until it was obvious there were no children there. On opening the door at the bottom of the stairs, 'the noise always stopped'. Both customers and staff saw a man behind the bar, sometimes in a white (medic's?) coat. One odd-job man 'refused to work in the bar on his own after seeing a group of children in very old-fashioned clothes playing in the pub'. The manager himself caught a flash of what he thought might be a 'child in a white apron'.

These experiences are particularly interesting once you are aware that this pub was originally built in 1898 as a 'Family Hospital' for the soldiers and families attached to the nearby Garrison, treating adults and children alike. [The pub has been The Garrison Arms since 2011]

(Reproduced with permission of Marian Livermore, editor of the *Shoebury Resident Magazine*.)

FAMILYS HOSPITAL, SHOEBURYNESS.

The Victorian Family's Hospital, Campfield Road, now The Garrison Arms. (Author's collection)

six

Unlikely Haunted Locations

Just when you thought every likely location had been exhausted ...

THE

HIPPODROME,

SOUTHEND-ON-SEA.

Managing Director ... Walter de Frece.
Resident Manager ... T. J. Robinson.

Two Performances Nightly,

6.50 and 9.0 p.m.

 ALWAYS

A STAR PROGRAMME.

Two Hours' Bright Varieties.

Popular Prices: 3d., 6d., 9d., 1s., 1s. 6d.
Boxes: 10s. 6d. and 15s.

PHONE : 333 SOUTHEND.

Typical programme for The Hippodrome, Southend.
(Author's collection)

Train between Southend Victoria and Rochford stations

Wesley Downes wrote of this unprecedented event in the now defunct *Ghosts and Hauntings*, in 1995, the magazine of which he was editor. The train was on the Southend Victoria to Shenfield line, in 1919, and was carrying a young man who had just taken his fiancée to the Edwardian Southend Hippodrome, then in Southchurch Road. He managed to catch the train by the skin of his teeth after seeing her home. As a result, he had no ticket, so when the ticket inspector walked into his compartment as the train reached Rochford, he indulged in desultory conversation with him while he wrote a receipt for the passenger's fare.

Further down the line, another ticket inspector shook the young man awake, asking to see his ticket. Alone in the carriage and half asleep, he explained the situation yet again, searching his pockets for the receipt. When he finally produced it and handed it over, the second inspector looked more than a little uncomfortable. 'Can you describe this other inspector?' he asked.

'He was about forty, clean-shaven, and, when he took his hat off, he revealed reddish hair and a large scar on his forehead.'

This description stunned the inspector; 'You have just described Ginger Rhodes, killed when he fell onto the railway line at Rayleigh trying to save a child.'

At that, both men looked even more closely at the handwritten receipt. 'God preserve us, I'll have to sit down. Look at this date,' said the inspector. The date read 24 December 1913.

They looked at each other, and the inspector produced his punch line, 'December 24th, 1913; Christmas Eve. That was the night Ginger was killed.'

Wesley cannot, now, recall his source, and the incident of the child's death on the rails at Rayleigh (on the same line) has not proved possible to track down. But his own comprehensive research and experience meant that he was happy to print this story as being a true account of the evening.

Rochford (Union) Hospital, Union Lane

On second thoughts, perhaps this is not such an unlikely site for a sighting (no pun intended) … i.e. a hospital is obviously a place where deaths are common.

In the 1920s, the *Southend Times* ran a whole series of leading articles about this hospital's resident ghost. The first report is from the 13 January 1923, when nurses had become perturbed by the constant wandering of a spectre at night, a spectre they had christened Matilda. It seems she was becoming more attention seeking, by ringing the bells that connected the night nurses with the patients' cubicles. Because she was dressed in nurse's uniform – albeit an old-fashioned version – she was not always identified as a ghost and had been mistaken from time to time as one of the staff in passing, until realisation dawned.

Interestingly, Matilda did not appear at any particular time, but was most often seen in one of the hospital corridors, along which she was seen to travel 'at breakneck speed' while doubled up rather like someone in pain. The nurses on night duty were becoming more and more nervous, and were refusing to sleep in certain cubicles or to frequent the corridors and stairs on their own.

Apart from the figure of Matilda, there were other paranormal goings-on – lights being lit and then extinguished without the intervention of any human hand, and a deep rumbling sound which inevitably heralded Matilda's appearance.

The matter was regarded with some scepticism by doctors and by the matron. Apart from the nature of the problem, the part of the premises frequented by Matilda was only around ten years old, and during its short history, there had been no untoward occurrence that might account for such activity. The official line was that the phenomena were the actions of a nurse or another practical joker. The nurses were not happy with this version of the events, however, and even the patients were said to believe that a ghost had indeed been present – some had even spoken to Matilda, although they received no response. The matron's decision was merely to improve the lighting in the passages.

As a result, an anonymous 'senior investigator' from the *Southend Times* decided to investigate the story further, and wrote of his findings a week later. Armed 'with a camera, a little logic and a sense of humour' his enquiries met with scepticism and no conclusion.

This story could have ended a week later, when a hospital attendant named Gell was

Rochford (Union) Hospital, as it was before the Second World War. (Author's collection)

summarily dismissed after admitting to dressing up in a white sheet and flitting around the hospital corridors at night as a 'harmless joke'. But it was not to be that simple. Gell had confessed to dressing up only once, after he had heard the reports of Matilda that were circulating, reports that he personally did not believe. He had been at the hospital for two years, but the ghost had been there for many more. Not only that, but Gell had not gone as far as dressing up as a nurse, and had been caught red- or perhaps white-handed. When it further transpired that sightings of Matilda had not ceased with his departure, another issue of the *Southend Times* on the 10 February led with 'Rochford Ghost is Very Much Alive'.

The Matilda story – but not necessarily Matilda's visitations – finished a week later, when another headline read 'Elusive Matilda'. It seems that the guardians of Rochford Union were now bent on ignoring her, in the hope that she would feel slighted and take herself off. It seems that this interesting ploy may indeed have worked!

This hospital became primarily a maternity unit in the 1950s, but many of the buildings have since been turned into apartments (including the listed boiler house, dating from 1933), following the expansion of the town's larger General Hospital in Prittlewell Chase. For the last few years, the re-vamped remains of Rochford (no longer Rochford Union) Hospital have taken in patients with mental health issues.

Southend Ambulance Headquarters, Prittlewell Chase

In May 1999, both the *Sunday Mirror* and the *Sunday People* gave space to some weird 'goings-on' in the ambulance-staff headquarters that were then attached to Southend Hospital, in Prittlewell Chase. Paramedic Colin Peagram is quoted as saying that the staff were 'petrified to be alone in the station at night' – because a figure had been seen drifting through a wall, voices had been heard in an empty room, and another figure had been seen standing by an ambulance but had then abruptly disappeared.

In addition, there were reports of windows and doors opening and closing – and stories of the 'ghost' answering the telephone even! At the time, the paramedics were considering calling in an exorcist, but whether they did so was not followed up by the press, and is not a matter of record in the hospital archives.

Old Dutch Barge, moored at Leigh-on-Sea

A little more recently, 2006, Nicky Alan, the star of Sky Real Lives' *Angels*, carried out an investigation with a team from EPIC (Extreme Paranormal Investigators Consortium). Nicky is a psychic medium from East London who was previously a police detective. She and her crew visited the barge as the result of a tip-off, and took plenty of equipment with them including cameras and camcorders.

After a quiet start, picking up little more than tappings, a massive floating orb was seen towards the bar area, and the photographer took several photographs. One of these revealed a hooded man in a cloak, but this photograph is sadly not suitable for reproduction. There was also a sighting of children, but too fleeting to describe and/or to have been photographed, but such is the nature of paranormal investigations.

The crew turned off the camcorder and left it on the bar while they investigated the top deck, from where they could hear loud banging. Frustratingly, they were unable to explain these particular sounds, but further orbs and tappings were experienced on the lower deck, and the team were generally happy with the spirit energy they attracted.

They were happier still when they viewed the camcorder footage, which was of interest because of the sounds recorded rather than the images. It seems that the camcorder had turned itself on again after they left the bar area, and there was the sound of someone bustling around the bar, and the sound of glasses clinking. There was then the distinctive sound of heavy footsteps crunching on gravel, before the machine turned itself off again. This footage has no rational explanation, and all the members of EPIC, and Nicky Alan herself, are convinced that this was a paranormal location.

Bus to Paglesham

In 2005, a driver, who was working on the last 10b run of the day to Paglesham East End, had a number of experiences, all in the same spot just after the road forks to Paglesham Church End. It seems that he was not the only driver, either.

Among them, they experienced a wide variety of phenomena; the engine of the bus would stall, the lights would go out, and a woman would be seen crossing the road before seemingly disappearing into the hedgerow at the side of the road. As a result of these experiences, this was not a favoured route, and drivers avoided it if they could.

Although this is not far from East Hall and the trees used by smugglers, featured in the *Open Spaces* section, the 'ghosts' do not seem to be linked.

seven

Phantom Dogs

It seems that, in the animal kingdom, it is largely dogs which 'return' after death – an occasional cat or horse perhaps might reappear, but it is mainly dogs. Man's best friend, yes, but with more in common than we might think.

Great Wakering

There is a fascinating audio cassette at Essex Record Office dating from 1970, recording the experiences of Leslie Cripps for the BBC. This was an elderly man who did not believe in ghosts and had always attributed any stories told to him as being due to the over excessive drinking of the storyteller.

However, he felt very differently when he had a (sober) experience himself, although he never mentioned the incident until he recorded this tape as he found it so hard to credit. He talks of a full moon on a slightly misty, windless Saturday evening around 9 p.m., when he was out to catch a rabbit or a duck down along the coast. Leslie had taken his gun and his friend's dog (Skip) into his car, arriving at around 10 p.m., when he could see the ripple of the incoming tide.

He alighted from his vehicle, walking along the ground, which had once been a store ground for the bricks made by kilns in the area, and saw a black-and-white dog bounding towards him. As he called out to Skip, he saw, to his astonishment, that the approaching dog was 2ft off the ground, and there was not a sound to be heard, not even his breathing. The dog galloped past him towards the sea and disappeared.

Two months later, Leslie visited the spot again, a little later in the evening, following a spell of rain. This time he was with his own dog, Nick, and was rubbing the dog dry in his estate wagon. Nick was obviously more sensitive than Skip because the hair on his body stiffened, as did his tail, and his gaze was fixed over his owner's shoulder. Leslie turned around and saw the very same dog, approaching in a semi-circular route from behind the car.

When he finally did mention it to a local friend, Tom, he said that he too had seen the dog but had been too 'scared' to tell anyone because 'no one would believe me'. If there were other witnesses, these too had kept quiet, but Leslie and Tom 'know what they saw'.

Apart from Leslie (and Tom), many others, past and present, have seen a black dog padding along Star Lane at night, *sans* owner and able to appear and disappear at will. The lane is named after a long-defunct inn, but the dog is less easy to explain.

This is not far away so could conceivably be the 'same' dog although the timing of the following incident is unclear. Issue no. 7 of *Ghosts and Hauntings* has an account of a man shooting on the marshes on a bright moonlit night, squatting down alongside one of the island's ponds.

The popular image of Black Shuck. (Image courtesy of www.clipart.com)

Something made him turn around, and he clearly saw, silhouetted against the moon, a large four-legged animal, larger than an Alsatian. Before he had time to react, the animal had disappeared.

However, on his way home, he again sensed something behind him, and re-loaded his gun promptly when he saw the same creature following him. He continued on his way, listening, until the sound of the padding footsteps stopped, upon which he turned – but there was nothing to be seen.

The next morning he decided to head back to the same spot to see if he could find any paw prints, or any tracks, but only found his own. He also reports that not a sound was heard, just like the dog that Leslie Cripps encountered.

Hockley and Hadleigh

The areas around Hockley Church and Hadleigh Castle have also spawned phantom-dog stories. If you see the former, with its fiery eyes, then you can apparently expect a year's bad luck, or worse. If the latter, sporting orange or red eyes and 'foaming at the mouth,' you can expect to meet with a tragic accident or nasty illness.

Note that the legend of the Black Dog, or Black Shuck, has been with us since the time of the Vikings, who brought stories of their Black Hound of Odin with them. Did they leave more than just stories behind with the Saxons, something more that haunts sites not far from their battle-grounds? Now, that is the question.

The moon across the marshes
The lonely Essex marshes
Through rotting bones of barges in the mud
The east wind calls the curlew
Who pipes his cry the same:
As when the river ran with Saxon blood
He rises from the blackness
And races through the lanes
To reach the lonely estuary track
And sneaks along the sea-walls,
The saltings and the flats
With no-one but the wind to call him back.

(From *Black Shuck* by Martin Newell, with his gracious permission)

Epilogue

Obviously, a lot of the stories in this book remain unexplained. I have not proved, to myself or anyone else, that there are ghosts – nor have I proved that they do not exist. I did not intend to do so either. I have, hopefully, however, sewed some doubt where there was none and provided some credible (or incredible!) explanations where there were none, with the aid not just of the spiritual and the psychic world but of the man/woman-in-the-street. I hope readers, resident or not, have enjoyed learning about a very different world – I have certainly enjoyed the leg-work and research involved in putting together this fascinating compendium. Southend-on-Sea, for me, has acquired a whole new dimension.

'There are more things in heaven and earth, Horatio. . .' from that early ghost story, *Hamlet*.

Dee Gordon, 2012

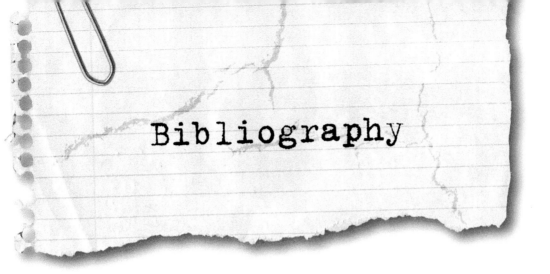

Bibliography

BOOKS

Day, J. Wentworth, *Ghosts and Witches* (Dorset Press, 1991)

Downes, W., *Memories of an Essex Ghost-Hunter* (Countryside Books, 2009)

Jerram-Burrows, L.E., *Rochford Remembers* (Rochford Hundred Historical Society, 1983)

King, C., *Haunted Essex* (The History Press, 2009)

Maple, E., *The Realm of Ghosts* (Robert Hale, 1964)

Morgan, G., *Secret Essex* (Ian Henry Publications, 1982)

Morgan, G., *Essex Witches* (Spur Books Ltd, 1973)

Newell, M., & Dodds, J., *Black Shuck* (Jardine Press, 1999)

Payne, J., *A Ghost Hunter's Guide to Essex* (Ian Henry Publications, 1987)

Pitt-Stanley, S., *Legends of Leigh* (Ian Henry Publications, 1989)

Puttick, B., *Ghosts of Essex* (Countryside Books, 1997)

Storey, N.R., *A Grim Almanac of Essex* (The History Press, 2005)

JOURNALS AND OTHER PUBLICATIONS

Essex Countryside (numerous issues)

Essex Life (numerous issues)

Essex Ghosts and Hauntings (all issues – published 1990s)

Ghosts and Hauntings (all issues – published 1990s)

Leigh Times (various issues)

Southend Echo (numerous issues)

Southend Observer (various issues)

Southend Pictorial (numerous issues)

Standard Recorder, Southend (numerous issues)

WEBSITES

www.arthurlloyd.co.uk

www.cannon.org.uk

www.clipart.com

www.essexparanormal.net

www.flickr.com

www.footstepsphotos.co.uk

www.ghosts-uk.net

www.ghosthuntersextraordinaire.co.uk

www.ghostseen.com

www.hauntedessex.com

www.hullbridgevillage.co.uk

www.mysterial.org.uk

http://naturalplane.blogspot.com

www.nickyalan.co.uk

www.paranormaldatabase.co.uk

www.psychicnights.com

www.s-o-sparanormal.co.uk

www.teaup.me.uk

OTHER

Ghosts of Essex (Felix Films, 2006)

Other titles published by The History Press

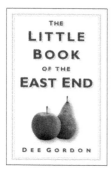

The Little Book of the East End
DEE GORDON

The Little Book of the East End is a funny, fast-paced, fact-packed compendium of the sort of frivolous, fantastic or simply strange information which no one will want to be without. Here we find out about the most unusual crimes and punishments, eccentric inhabitants, famous sons and daughters and literally hundreds of wacky facts. A reference book and a quirky guide, this can be dipped in to time and time again to reveal something new about the East End. A wonderful package and essential reading for visitors and locals alike.

978 0 7524 5717 8

Southend at War
DEE GORDON

Dee Gordon's book is the unique and fascinating result of many conversations with people about the lives of their families in Southend during the First and Second World War. Vivid memories are recounted, including interviews with former Land Army girls, evacuees, and members of the Home Guard. Illustrated with over 90 archive photographs and documents, *Southend at War* draws on the first-hand accounts of those who were present during those dangerous years and is sure to appeal to everyone interested in the history of Southend.

978 0 7524 5262 3

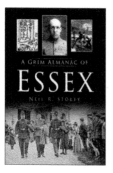

A Grim Almanac of Essex
NEIL R. STOREY

Matthew Hopkins, the Witchfinder-General, was born at Manningtree in the 1620s, Dick Turpin, the country's most notorious highwayman, was born at Thaxted in 1705 and the nation's longest serving hangman, William Calcraft, was born at Little Baddow near Chelmsford. Neil Storey's macabre calendar chronicles the darker side of life in Essex. Murderers and footpads, pimps and prostitutes, riots, rebels, bizarre funerals, disaster and peculiar medicine all feature. If you have the stomach for it, then read on.

978 0 7524 6510 4

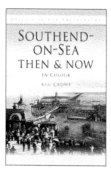

Southend-on-Sea Then & Now
KEN CROWE

Southend-on-Sea has gone through many transformations since its birth in the Middle Ages, when a settlement of farmers and fishermen was established at the southernmost end of the lands of Prittlewell Priory. Having acquired the name 'South End', the area changed when the Lord of the Manor in the eighteenth century had a 'New Town' built along the cliffs to the west. In this fascinating photographic history, Ken Crowe takes a fond look at his home town, exploring the changes to its streets through carefully chosen snapshots of Southend-on-Sea as it was in the past and is today.

978 0 7524 6323 0

Visit our website and discover thousands of other History Press books.

www.thehistorypress.co.uk